The Boy Inside

An Asperger's Syndrome Success Story

By Rhonda Jones Vardeman

"For I know the plans I have for you," declares the Lord, "plans to prosper you and not to harm you, plans to give you hope and a future." Jeremiah 29:11 (The Holy Bible, New International Version)

Front cover illustration and Foreword by Eric Vardeman

In loving memory of Eric's grandparents, Curtis and Merle Jones, Uncle Leon Roberts, and Richard Maple, the greatest tutor in the world.

Some of the names in this story have been changed. It is not the intent of this book to make anyone look bad or to cast a negative light on anyone. The only persons whose names have been changed are the few children who were unkind to Eric when he was young.

I wish to thank several people who helped provide information for this book or who had a positive influence on Eric during his life: Grandmother and Papa Bear Jones, Gee-Gah and Papa Vardeman, Aunt Bunk (Annette) Roberts and Uncle Leon, Aunt Amy Lawler, Uncle Don and Aunt Weezie (Louise) Jones, Aunt Beth James, Dr. Rita Horton, the Rev. Frances Attaway, the Rev. Charles Humphreys, Dr. Juliet Spencer, Dr. Perry Hill, Laurie Nussbaum, Jo Linn Burt, the teachers at North Highlands Methodist Pre-School, the teachers and staff at Blanchard Elementary School, University Christian Prep and Calvary Baptist Academy, Richard and Martha Maple, and the tutors and staff at The Reading Center of Shreveport.

And to my editor and friend, Sallie Rose Hollis, heartfelt thanks for your editing expertise. I could not have written this book without your help.

Rhonda Jones Vardeman

Contents

Foreword

Out of her great love for me, my mother wrote *The Boy Inside*, a book about my experiences living with Asperger's Syndrome, an autism spectrum disorder. When I was very young, I behaved oddly and had OCD symptoms, obsessing over things such as strings, ceiling fans and animal tails. This disorder prevented me from thinking about things that a child should focus on in his young life—playtime, schoolwork and building relationships with friends and family.

Concerned that I would never have a normal life, my parents vowed to turn things around and went into action to get help for me. They turned to child and adolescent psychiatrist Dr. Rita Horton, reading tutor Richard Maple, psychologist Dr. Perry Hill and licensed clinical social worker Laurie Nussbaum. These people were some of the professionals who made a difference in my life, helping me overcome my setbacks. My extended family as well as my church family and friends also were supportive in my struggle to live beyond the limits of a syndrome that had kept me bottled up and socially handicapped.

Armed with tools for success, I worked hard, prayed hard and increased my desire to overcome obstacles that had prohibited me from living the life of a normal child. Gradually, the odd, introverted boy came out and saw his potential. I made friends, improved my grades and thought about my future. I graduated from high school with good grades and a desire to go to college. Always having had a fondness for the outdoors and animals, I decided to study wildlife habitat management. I am a senior at Louisiana Tech University in Ruston and have two college scholarships.

I encourage anyone who is struggling with OCD symptoms or any autism-related disorder to research the resources available and get help as quickly as possible. I found hope and comfort in these simple but powerful words from Philippians 4:13: *All things are possible through Christ who strengthens me.*

Thank you for your interest in my mother's book. It is a thorough look at my life from birth through high school graduation. A stickler for details, my mother covers everything—even those embarrassing incidents that I would rather forget! I hope it will make you laugh, cry and, more importantly, realize that no obstacle is too difficult to overcome.

Eric A. Vardeman, October 2011

Some Resources Available

Asperger's Syndrome and Other Autism Spectrum Disorders

There are many places to turn for assistance for persons diagnosed with Asperger's Syndrome and other autism spectrum disorders. A few of the many centers and associations are listed below:

Office of Special ducation Programs of the U.S. Department of Education (OSEP) – Washington, D.C.

National Dissemination Center for Children with Disabilities (NICHCY) – Washington, D.C.

Asperger Syndrome Coalition of the U.S., Inc. – Jacksonville, Fla.

Autism Research Institute, San Diego, Calif.

National Autism Association, Nixa, Missouri

Consider attending seminars, symposiums or conferences that might be offered. These venues often feature guest speakers who are professionals in the areas of behavior modification, autism spectrum disorders and other related topics.

Find a health care professional who will meet the needs of the individual.

Speak to teachers and counselors if the individual is a school student.

Read newspaper and magazine articles and books on the subject. There are many available. One excellent book is Tony Attwood's *Asperger's Syndrome: a guide for parents and professionals.*

Start or join a support group in your city or town with other individuals who have family members or friends with similar disorders. The group will be invaluable for sharing information and providing a listening ear.

Share with a church's small group.

Research the Internet to locate other resources.

Chapter One

An Interesting Lad

Eric's small, fat hands captured the piece of lint and held it as if it were a precious stone. He had started crawling and, like many other babies, had begun to investigate objects. His fascination, however, was on tiny things: pieces of lint, a short string or other small object. Even before he could crawl, he would rub his baby blanket in the same place until a tiny "pill" would come off. Then he would rub it between his thumb and forefinger. Whether it was a "pill" from a blanket or a piece of lint or string, Eric would study the object for quite some time, causing his dad and me to believe he had great concentration at such a young age. We didn't realize that his keen sense of concentration was indicative of something else—a problem.

Eric ate well, slept well, smiled and laughed. He was a happy baby and we were happy parents. He was delivered by Caesarean section at Schumpert Medical Center in Shreveport, Louisiana, by Dr. Susan Shattuck on a cool March morning in 1990. Eric was turned the wrong way in the womb, and after unsuccessful attempts by Dr. Shattuck to turn him around, his heartbeat slowed, and the decision was made to perform the C-section. He was the first grandchild on my side of the family to be born since 1976, and the first on my husband Rob's side of the family since 1985. Needless to say, he was very well loved, a bit spoiled and definitely doted on, particularly by his grandparents. We were all blessed to have him.

We had decided that I would continue working full-time at Arkla Energy Resources in downtown Shreveport. Rob and I had talked to my sister, Annette Roberts, about keeping Eric for us and she had agreed. I knew he would be in excellent hands and that he would learn a lot from her and her husband, Leon, a great guy who spent a lot of time outdoors keeping his slightly more than six acres of land in prime condition, helping his neighbors, taking care of his garden and tinkering on his 1953 vintage Chevy pickup.

So after my six-week maternity leave was over, I went back to work, dropping Eric off at Annette's house in the mornings and picking him up there in the afternoons.

As Eric grew in length and weight, so did his fascination for tiny objects. He loved to touch things, and once I caught him "digging" in one of my ivy plants. His little hands had dug a fairly significant-sized hole in the dirt by moving his fingers back and forth. I'm sure my sister had to watch him closely to make sure those little hands were kept out of harm's way.

Before Eric could talk, he let us know he was disturbed by certain things. If one sun visor on the car was down, he would point to the other one and make "uh-uh" sounds until we pulled the other visor down. The visors either had to both be down or up; if they weren't, he would be upset until we corrected the imbalance. The same thing was true for chairs being pushed up under the table. All of the chairs needed to be pushed under the table or he would get upset. After he began putting sentences together, Eric would verbalize what he saw as a problem. He was bothered if all of the cabinet doors were not closed. Even when someone was taking something out or putting something up, he would say, "Shut that cabinet." My sister recalls one such incident when she was in the midst of cooking, and she had opened a cabinet to get something out of it. Eric pointed out to her that she had not shut the cabinet door. "Just a minute, Sweetie, and I'll close it," Annette told him. Tears welled up right away in Eric's eyes, and she dropped whatever she was doing. "I ran and closed it," she remembered. If lights were burned out, Eric couldn't rest until we changed the bulbs. He was bothered by things that were not aligned properly, such as a door that might not have been hung properly and had more space on one side or the other at the top or bottom. He would squat down and study a door for several minutes and then let us know if it wasn't right.

By the time he was two, Eric knew the alphabet. Rob's dad, Alex Vardeman, had printed from a computer program in large block print each letter of the alphabet, and we used it as a border in Eric's room, hanging it low enough for him to touch while standing on his bed. The high-pitched voice with a slight Southern drawl would announce "A, B, C," etc., until he made it through every letter. He also knew each letter out of sequence and could repeat the alphabet backward. Wow, he's brilliant, we thought.

We weren't the only ones who thought he was smart. I had taken Eric to the grocery store when he was still small enough to ride in the basket of the grocery cart. We were in the produce section when Eric pointed to the bananas and proclaimed, "Del Monte." Another shopper looked at me with surprise and said, "He can read!"

"Well," I confessed, "he knows the label for Del Monte," although I wanted to say, "Yes, he can. He's brilliant."

It was about this time in Eric's life he began his fascination with ceiling fans. He would study a fan as its blades circled round and round and keep his eyes on it for several minutes. "That fan is on medium," he would say. He became an expert on fans and their speeds. We would go to a restaurant, and if a fan was not on, he would tell the waiter to "turn that fan on," or if the fan was on, he'd say, "Turn that fan on medium." It was funny but a little embarrassing. My husband and I are both a little on the shy side, so when Eric would make a demand like that, we would tell the waiter, "That's ok, you don't have to turn the fan on." The waiter usually would oblige, though, because the little guy was just so cute. Eric's fascination with fans continued for some time and included his knowing how many blades each fan in our house had as well as my sister's house, and both sets of grandparents' homes. Usually he wanted all the fans on all the time. He also named the fans at my sister's house. I remember the names of two of them: "Beaver and One" was the fan in her youngest son's room, and one of the other fans was called "Branches Branches." The only thing we can think of as to why he gave them such strange names is that it might have had something to do with the sound the fans made as the blades were spinning around. At about age two and a half, Eric began carrying around a chain or string, pretending to turn on his fan. He also began to move his right hand around in a circular motion to mimic the motion of fan blades turning. The speed of Eric's hand moving around depended on whether the "fan" was set on slow, medium or high. Ryan, a friend of my sister's middle son, nicknamed him "Fan on Medium" and would call Eric by that name whenever he was around him.

Eric later added a blade of grass, his shirt tail, a play telephone cord and Mardi Gras beads (he called them "beebs") to the list of items he would carry around. The pulling evolved into twirling, and then he added singing to the process. He would march around twirling the object and singing a song. He would say, "This is the first song," and then would go through about 10 or 12 songs before he would stop. This behavior would happen inside the house or outside in the yard or in the car or while we visited friends and neighbors. I'm sure many people who witnessed this were too kind to tell us this was bizarre behavior. We knew it was bizarre, but there wasn't much we thought we could do about it. Eric seemed to stress out if he wasn't able to finish his song list.

Rob's sister Beth James recalled when he would make clay "snakes," lining them up on the living room floor at his grandparents' home. Each snake would represent a song, and the length of a song would determine the length of the "snake."

Eric's love of music continued as he became introduced to different types of music. Rob and I both love music and play instruments. We also have a 1961 Wurlitzer jukebox that Eric enjoyed. Before he learned to walk, Eric would pull himself up to the jukebox and bend his knees to the beat. He especially loved "Green Onions" by Booker T and the MGs. "Hey, the little guy's got rhythm," we observed.

During his introduction to listening to various types of music, Eric began to enjoy listening to a Three Dog Night compact disc that I had. *The Best of Three Dog Night* contains 20 of the group's greatest hits, and Eric soon learned the names of all the songs. But that wasn't all he learned. He could name the songs in order from first to last, from last to first and tell us the title of the eighth song, the fourteenth song, etc. He exhibited peculiar

15

behavior in many ways, but he certainly had a gift in the rote memory department. He also pointed out whether the song ended at once or faded out by saying either the song had "an over" or it didn't have "an over."

One thing that bothered us was that Eric couldn't sit still and watch a cartoon or anything else on television. He seemed to have no interest in focusing on something that wasn't in his hands. He loved books, however, and would sit still when I read his favorite books to him. Some of these books I read to him several times in a row. Someone told us it is natural for a child to want the same books read to him, so we didn't worry too much about it and were glad he loved books. He had several favorites, but the two I'll never forget are *The Going To Bed Book* by Sandra Boynton and *One Little Teddy Bear* by Mark Burgess. Eric memorized both of the books and could look at the pictures and "read" the books to me.

When we visited my sister and her family at Thanksgiving when Eric was about two and a half years old, he spent most of the time running around in circles in the living room. We couldn't get him to stop. He was over-stimulated with so many people around. We noticed the same behavior when we had visitors at our house. He ran in circles in whatever room we were in.

Eric always had an aversion to loud noises, although "fear" might be a better word for it. He had never liked the sound of the vacuum cleaner, and I would schedule vacuuming the floor when he was taking his naps. Then, another noise began to bother him, even though it was not nearly as loud as the sound the vacuum cleaner made on the carpet. Eric's new fear was the sound of soft-serve ice cream machines. There was one at a family-style restaurant in Vivian, Louisiana, and one at a cafeteria in Ruston, Louisiana. Eric was with my parents and sister on one occasion and with Rob and his parents at the other one. In both cases, Eric had to be taken out of the restaurant because he was screaming and out of control.

In December 1992, I suffered a miscarriage. Rob and I were devastated. I as in my fourth month, and there had been no signs of a problem. However, when I went in for my monthly appointment with Dr. Shattuck, she couldn't detect a heartbeat and quickly prepared the ultrasound machine. The ultrasound confirmed Dr. Shattuck's fear and mine, too. She comforted me and then said, "Rhonda, here is a phone so you can call your husband." That was one phone call I did not want to make. I remember thinking I wish she would call him. I just didn't want to tell him we had lost the baby. I finally made the call, and Rob arrived at the doctor's office a few minutes later. We drove home, taking turns crying. That's the only time I remember seeing my husband cry. I called my mother after we got home, and Rob did the same with his mom. The next few days and weeks were tough, but we relied on our faith, family and friends to see us through.

A couple of days after we learned of the miscarriage, my sister told me a precious story about Eric. After I had called my mother to tell her the sad news, she, in turn, called my sister to tell her. Eric was at her house because it was a weekday and she was keeping him while I was at work. He was in the room when the call came in, and my sister said she was saying things like, "oh, no," and "I'm so sorry" into the phone receiver. Annette never mentioned anything about a baby or me. After she hung up the phone, Eric—who had no idea he was going to be a big brother—said, "That little baby is with God in heaven."

I can only believe that somehow God spoke to him and gave Eric some type of understanding that only the Lord Himself can accomplish. There is no explanation for what happened other than it was divine intervention. If there was anything good that came out of the loss of that child, it was the blessing of that wonderful story involving Eric and our Creator.

Chapter Two

Pre-School and a Baby Brother

At age three, Eric started pre-school at North Highlands Elementary Pre-school at North Highlands United Methodist Church in Shreveport. Pre-school was three days a week—Monday, Wednesday and Friday—for three hours a day, nine to noon. I'm not sure who cried more on the first day—Eric or me. I was almost to the point of deciding he was too young to start pre-school when my sister encouraged me to leave him there, assuring me he would be all right. She knew all about little boys and "taking baby steps" with them. She had reared three boys herself and had been through all sorts of things with them. "He'll be fine," she told me. Carla Shands, the teacher of the three-year-olds, pulled Eric up on her lap and started talking to him. With a reassuring look at me, she let me know she would do her part in making him feel comfortable. Nonetheless, I cried all the way to work. Rob called me after picking Eric up from his first day at pre-school and told me Eric didn't want to leave. "I want to go back there again sometime," Eric told Rob. I was thrilled and very relieved.

Eric seemed to enjoy pre-school, but he didn't always like to participate in the class' various activities. He also did not identify with the other children on a peer level. He was more of an observer than a participant. Although my friend's son was in the same class and Eric knew him, he wasn't interested in playing with Forest or any of the other children. In his role as an observer, Eric could tell us everything that happened at school—from who cried to who had to spend a few minutes in timeout to who got sick and threw up. He seemed to be grasping some of the lessons, too. He could sing all of the songs the class learned and would repeat them at home. In fact, he would sing the same songs so often that we noticed it was difficult to get him to do anything else. While he made progress in some areas, there were certain tasks such as coloring and cutting with scissors that he didn't grasp. One day after pre-school when I picked up Eric and another child who was in a carpool with us, the little friend made fun of the way Eric colored his pictures. "He can't color. Eric just scribble-scrabbles," he criticized. "Eric doesn't like to color," I replied, trying to convince myself that's all there was to the problem. Denial played a big part of how both Rob and I coped with Eric and his strange ways. We knew he was smart in some areas, and he continued to amaze us with his memorization skills. But we also knew he wasn't like other kids. Would he grow out of it? We certainly hoped so.

One evening after school, I received a call from Mrs. Shands, Eric's teacher. After a few minutes of conversation, she told me about an incident involving Eric that had happened that day at school. Her classroom had an air conditioning vent that ran alongside one wall. Small screws held part of the metal vent in place, and Eric had somehow unscrewed all four screws and brought them to her. Mrs. Shands said she had no idea how Eric unscrewed them but she wanted us to know what had happened. I apologized and told her I would talk with him about what he had done. Rob and I figured that the screws must not have been tightened and were loose enough for Eric to unscrew with his small fingers. At least he gave the screws to his teacher instead of losing them or putting them in his mouth.

We were preoccupied with Eric and his adventures in pre-school, so it came as somewhat of a surprise and a great blessing to find out that we were going to have another child. We were a little nervous because of the miscarriage, but our faith was strong, and we badly wanted another baby. The same day Eric turned four, his little brother, Kurt, was born.

We did the best we could to prepare Eric for the birth of his little brother. The hospital had a class for big brothers- and sisters-to-be, and they got to dress in scrubs and ride around on a gurney. They visited the window of the maternity ward where they peeked in at the babies in their tiny bassinettes. We got Eric a special button that said, "I'm the big brother," and he wore the button to school on his birthday. Later that day, Rob brought him up to the hospital to see Kurt. I couldn't wait to see him and find out what he thought of his little brother, also born by C-Section.

Eric came into the hospital room, bypassed Kurt in the bassinette and headed straight for the lamp beside my bed, where he proceeded to turn the light bulb off and on. Over and over and over. Rob finally had to distract him and draw his attention to his new baby brother. Eric's reaction was typical of many older brothers and sisters—he didn't give the baby the time of day. He had bigger fish to fry. There were lights to be turned on and off, strings to twirl and songs to sing. Although he never hurt or threatened his brother, Eric treated Kurt more like an object to be ignored until Kurt got old enough to play. One of our favorite "Eric quotes" came after Kurt got a little bigger and Eric realized that maybe he was a little fun to have around. "I hope Kurt lasts a long time," he told Rob and me. "If you take good care of him, he will," I said, winking at Rob.

When Kurt was four months old, I quit working full-time and began a new career as a stay-at-home mom, only to discover the term "stay-at-home mom" is widely overused and very incorrectly depicts what a parent does when she chooses not to work full-time. With two children at home, I often found myself loading them both up in my Honda Prelude and taking them to the store or gas station or on other errands. The older they got, the busier I got because of school and their activities.

Even though I loved taking care of the boys, I was not very comfortable being unemployed, so I began working part-time at Mother's Day Out at our church. It was summertime, so I had both Eric and Kurt with me. This two-day-a-week job was probably the hardest work I've ever had, and I would come home exhausted after only five hours. It was draining trying to keep up with my own children, but when there were others for whom I had a responsibility, I really had to keep on my toes.

The next year when Eric was in four-year-old pre-school, his coloring skills still were lacking. In September 1994, the class was given a math skills sheet to color and practice writing the numeral "10." "How many monkeys are in the trees? Write the numeral," were the instructions. Eric took a purple crayon and colored haphazardly all over the center of the page. Most of his work was done in much the same way. Soon I received a note from his teacher, Anne Oliver, who suggested that Eric work every day with coloring, using scissors to cut shapes and numbers, putting puzzles together and other activities that would improve his skill in using his hands. We worked with Eric every day, but it wasn't easy getting his attention or keeping it for any length of time. He seemed to be making some progress, but one evening in the spring Mrs. Oliver called me and asked if we could have a conference about Eric. She gently and kindly told me that Eric was immature, was off-task on certain skills and suggested that he repeat four-year-old pre-school. She said she felt he was not ready to start kindergarten in the fall and wanted to reserve Eric a spot in her class if we would like to have him repeat it. I wasn't sure how to react to the news, but told her that I would talk it over with Rob and would get back with her. I'm sure I probably cried after hanging up the phone. *Couldn't other people see how smart Eric was? Why did his teacher think he needed to be held back just because he was a little different?* Besides, we had talked with him about going to a new school the next year, and he already was getting used to the idea.

I reiterated my conversation with Mrs. Oliver to my mother-in-law, Mary Vardeman. A retired school teacher and counselor, she listened and then made what turned out to be the best suggestion thus far in Eric's life. After noting Eric's strengths and abilities, she said we might want to call the Caddo Parish School Board psychologist for advice. She then wrote some notes for me:

o/c (obsessive-compulsive) behavior? Visors in car, Fans (twirling began), String – music (sometimes accompanied by walking or humming or strumming). Visual/motor difficulty – cutting, coloring in lines, puzzles, copying triangles, squares, etc., no interest in TV.

Plays alongside other children, not with others. Advanced verbal skills – loves books, large vocabulary, retells stories, asks lots of why and what if questions about events and stories.

21

Displays sense of humor. Loves animals, interested in nature.

I made the call to the psychologist and mentioned the items my mother-in-law had written. The psychologist recommended I call Dr. Rita Horton, a child and adolescent psychiatrist, because she said what I was describing sounded like attention deficit disorder (ADD) which, if diagnosed, would need to be treated with medication that only a psychiatrist or another M.D. could dispense. I couldn't imagine putting our child on medication. He had just turned five. *There must be something else that can be done for him, I thought.*

Chapter Three

A Psychiatrist Enters the Picture

After much thought and prayer, we decided to let Eric start kindergarten at Blanchard Elementary School in the fall. Our first appointment with Dr. Horton was during the summer before school began in 1995. Rob and I were apprehensive about the appointment. *What if Eric didn't act the way he normally does? What if the doctor doesn't notice anything unusual? What would we do then?* Eric didn't disappoint us. Apparently he was as comfortable in front of Dr. Horton as he was at home. He found a string and began to twirl it and sing while marching around. Dr. Horton observed Eric for almost an hour.

"He is not autistic," Dr. Horton said. "He's far too connected to other people." She spoke in generalities about children who have disorders and gave us hope that Eric could be helped. "It's bad when the child wants to stop (obsessive behavior) and can't. We don't want this behavior to take over his life." I was thinking it already had, but I felt there finally was hope for Eric and for us in dealing with it. Dr. Horton said obsessive behavior is part of a wide spectrum of disorders. She mentioned the word "perseverate" and that it means forgetting to forget and, thus, there is repetitive behavior. There were not a lot of studies on medication for children, Dr. Horton explained, and if she put Eric on any medication, it would be on a trial basis only. Believing that it was too soon to put him on medication without observing Eric further, Dr. Horton said she wanted to see Eric a couple of times before she took that step. I kept thinking that I didn't want him to take medication, but I trusted that Dr. Horton, in her experience with children and various disorders, knew what was best.

Before we left her office, Dr. Horton gathered other information from us after she spent some time with Eric alone. We talked about family history, when Eric's symptoms and odd behavior began, whether anyone in either of our families exhibited unusual behavior or tics, his relationship with his little brother, any fears such as germs, if everything had to be in place in a room, if there were rituals Eric had when he went through doorways, if he checked behind himself after doing something, any allergies, any medication he was already taking, who his pediatrician was and my history of pregnancies. Through her few minutes with Eric alone, she observed his walking on tiptoes, which he had done for some time. She learned some other things, too.

"Which one of you is the musician?" Dr. Horton asked. Apparently Eric had talked to her about our guitars and piano as well as the music played on our stereo system. "Eric talked about 'Wasted Time (Reprise)'," she said. He probably also told her it is the fifth song from The Eagles' *Hotel California* album and is the song in between "Wasted Time" and "Victim of Love."

Following another appointment with Dr. Horton, she prescribed a small amount of Prozac every other day for Eric to see if it would curtail the obsessive-compulsive disorder (OCD) behavior that was getting in his way. At that time, I didn't even know that Prozac came in liquid form or was ever given to a child that young. As difficult as it was for us as parents to give our five-year-old child a drug that is popularly used to treat depression, we were anxious to try something that might help Eric live as normal a life as possible. The Prozac doses would take a few days to be effective, Dr. Horton explained, because it has a long half-life, meaning it takes several doses to get into the system as well as taking several days to wear off.

In addition to the medication, we were urged to try behavior modification on Eric. We would give him a time limit on playing with strings. Rob came up with the idea of setting the kitchen timer for Eric, allowing him only a few minutes at a time to play with his string. Eric didn't like having a timer set on his repetitive habit, so usually he would stop on his own before the timer sounded, or he would decide to not play with the string at all. Although it became easier to persuade him to stop twirling strings, we could tell the desire was still there. Eric understood we would like for him to stop, and he said things he knew we wanted to hear:

"I don't want to play with strings any more. I'm just going to play with toys." He still needed to be reassured that we loved him, though, because he once asked his daddy, "If I play with strings, will you still love me?" Rob reassured him that we would always love him no matter what he did. Even when he was at that young age of five, Eric wanted to do the right thing but wanted to make sure that we loved him if he couldn't stop the habit. It was sad because he wanted to please us yet he still had strong urges for the repetitive behavior. Looking back on it, I can't imagine what he must have been going through.

Dr. Horton asked us to get back to her after Eric took the Prozac for a week. I kept notes in order to give a more complete report. The notes, typed and faxed to Dr. Horton, are as follows:

Notes on Eric A. Vardeman

Birthdate: March 14, 1990

Thursday, July 20, 1995 – ¼ tsp. Prozac Liquid

Notable quote: "I just like to play by myself. I don't want to play with anyone."

Rested about 1:30 p.m. but didn't take nap.

Rob made a videotape of Eric playing with a string and going through his list of "songs."

Friday, July 21, 1995

Nothing unusual noted for the day; last day of swimming lessons. (His eyes are very sensitive to the light when he's at the pool); holds his hands over them most of the time).

Saturday, July 22, 1995 – ¼ tsp. Prozac Liquid

Noticed jacket with string missing from coat rack by the door. Is in the habit of playing with jacket string daily.

Has been calling himself "Case" and says he doesn't like children. (Seems as if he's had a truth serum).

Sunday, July 23, 1995

Eric slept with his ceiling fan on last night for the first time in a very long time. Saturday night told his grandmother, "Sometimes I don't even like to play with strings." This was after he became upset when he wanted to play with his brother's pacifier holder string, and his grandmother tried to get his mind off of it. She finally cut a piece of string for him to play with and he did for only a few minutes.

Eric was sick with a stomach ache and vomited once tonight. Felt a lot better after that and drank some Sprite.

Monday, July 24, 1995 – ¼ tsp. Prozac Liquid

Ate a regular breakfast. Went to library program at Blanchard Library; went swimming at neighbor's pool; played only a few minutes with string today.

Tuesday, July 25, 1995

Not hungry for breakfast at home; ate about 10 a.m. at grandmother's house; rest of day fairly normal activity; went swimming. Today has been calling himself "Purple."

Does not like for us to set the timer on him for time he can play with a string. Will put string away rather than have timer set.

Wednesday, July 26, 1995 – ¼ tsp. Prozac Liquid

Didn't eat much breakfast today; said medicine left a bad taste in his mouth (has not complained until today about the taste; we've not added the grape flavor).

Wanted to play with string, and I offered to set timer. Eric objected to the timer.

Played with string for 5 minutes. Didn't want to put it away until I offered to set timer again. He put it away.

Called Dr. Horton with report; she said to continue medicine as directed.

Tonight up late because went to airport to meet Eric's Aunt Beth and cousin Emmy from California. Was tired.

Thursday, July 27, 1995

Has been lethargic today; went to Mother's Day Out at the church and did some drawing, played with clay, had limited outside activity because of the heat; did not eat very well today or tonight.

Visited with out-of-town relatives at his grandmother's house most of the afternoon; put puzzles together, looked at his favorite books and played in the sprinkler; rested a good bit.

We're noticing a slight decrease in appetite and a good bit of resting which is unusual for Eric; he's usually on the move all day. His appetite is normally consistently inconsistent—at times he eats a lot for a few days, and other times he doesn't eat much.

We had an appointment with Dr. Horton on August 9 and reported we had removed potential strings from our house so Eric wouldn't be tempted to "twirl." When he did play with strings, he could stop without difficulty. However, Dr. Horton noticed something new that Eric was doing—twisting his hair. She observed him walking on his toes and pacing a lot and noted that at some point, he would need occupational therapy for his gait as well as speech evaluation for his articulation deficits. He had a slight lisp due to a cross-bite. Dr. Horton noted that Eric was cheerful and rather chatty, saying things like, "I'm a doctor. I'm a girl named Crystal. These are my paws." That day Eric's imagination was in full swing.

Chapter Four

Kindergarten Issues

Eric started to kindergarten on August 17, and we talked with his teacher, Emma Scott, as soon as we could about our child. During the three weeks before our next appointment with Dr. Horton, we were receiving notes almost daily from Miss Scott. Unfortunately, they were not the kind of notes parents like to receive from teachers. These notes described how Eric was "off task" with his assignments, seemed to be very immature, and he was focusing on things that were not relevant. One of Miss Scott's notes read:

Mrs. Vardeman,

Eric's attention span is very short. He is off task with all assignments. I am monitoring him and will talk to you about his behavior soon. I have noticed that any time a transition is made, for example, from math to writing, it totally throws him off. Or if we have been in the room all day and that afternoon we have to go to gym or music, it disrupts his whole schedule.

Although the notes were upsetting, we appreciated having them because it was information Dr. Horton needed in order to treat Eric's case.

After we shared the notes with Dr. Horton, she smiled and commented that at least Miss Scott didn't say he was marching around twirling a string.

Miss Scott continued to keep us up-to-date on our son's behavior and his work progress by sending us notes. *Practice coloring. Eric is having a hard time adjusting. As time goes on, I hope it will get better.* A September progress report read: *I have to work with Eric one-on-one most of the time.* A few days later, Miss Scott wrote: *Mrs. Vardeman, Eric is doing better. He is getting adjusted. However, I do have to stay close to him to keep him on task.* Another note read, *Continue to practice coloring. Eric was more on task today.* Each of the progress reports had a minus next to "works neatly."

Eric's repetitive tendencies were becoming more infrequent, but his attention was inadequate. Dr. Horton diagnosed Eric with attention deficit hyperactivity disorder (ADHD) and decided to try Ritalin to help with that problem. She was cautious, however, because of not knowing how the combination of Ritalin and Prozac would affect Eric. "It can tip the balance," Dr. Horton explained. "We want him to be able to sleep and eat." She told us to be aware of any change in behavior and mood. Watch for hyper-activity or the opposite effect of slowing down, she said. We learned from Dr. Horton that even though Ritalin can help with focusing problems, too much Ritalin can cause hyperactivity. Dr. Horton wanted our five-year-old to have the right combination.

Rob and I met with Miss Scott a few days after the appointment with Dr. Horton to check his progress. His teacher had told Rob's sister, Amy, who also taught kindergarten at Blanchard Elementary, that Eric was "coming along." Amy watched out for Eric and gave us regular reports. It was great to have an inside track with Amy, and Miss Scott was kind enough to let Amy know what was going on with Eric. We learned at our meeting with Miss Scott that Eric was indeed coming along with his attention and was getting more on task with his work. However, we were disappointed to learn that our little fellow was not interacting with his classmates. We were hoping the medication would help him in that area, too. "He mostly will walk around (at recess) and will play on pieces of equipment (by himself)," Miss Scott told us.

There was one classmate whom Eric began to talk about—Trenton—who was a rather large-for-his-age student. After a while, we learned the two classmates would play chase and have some interaction. We were happy with that news. Trenton, however, would tend to get into trouble for talking or other kindergarten misdemeanors. One afternoon, Eric came home from school with a folded note pinned to his shirt. *I wonder what this is all about*, I thought, as I removed the note and opened it. The note began, "Mrs. Livingston, Trenton has been acting up in class. Please call me as soon as possible so we can discuss this." It was signed, "Miss Scott." I questioned Eric about the note. "How did it get pinned to your shirt?" It took some time, but I finally learned that Trenton's older sister had pinned the note to Eric in the gym before the bell rang. I guess she didn't want her brother to get in trouble. The incident was funny, but it also worried Rob and me because we didn't know what to expect from Eric. He was so trusting, and every situation was different. We could tell him not to let anyone except a teacher or other adult pin a note to his shirt, but that only covers one situation. *What about all of the other things that could happen? How do you cover everything?*

Eric's first progress report in October still had a minus next to "works neatly." Miss Scott wrote: *He's trying very hard; Sometimes he gets in a hurry.* The next couple of weeks, she reported, "doing better" and "trying hard." Other October progress reports said Eric was doing better with neatness, but he "tends to get confused and distracted when in a large group."

At our next visit with Dr. Horton we had some good things to report in that Eric seemed to be showing steady improvement in his behavior and with his schoolwork. "He's back on track developmentally," Dr. Horton explained, but cautioned that if he began to slip off track, to let her know before it became habitual. We learned that as Eric grew and gained weight, he probably would outgrow the dose of medicine. "We want steady improvement," she said.

Discipline was a difficult area for us when it came to Eric. It wasn't that we didn't believe in it, but it was so hard to decide how to administer it. Give him two choices when possible, Dr. Horton explained, and let Eric make decisions and have some control. And always let him know there are consequences for misbehaving. That was great advice for any parent.

During the spring of 1996, Eric was given an assignment to dictate a story to his parents to write. Eric wrote about one of his favorite places to go, the woods across the street from our house. Titled, "My Favorite Woods," here is his story:

My Favorite Woods

By: Eric Vardeman

I like to go on a trail in the woods. I like to go through a long trail, sometimes a short trail. I like to go in the tree house. It's mine and Christen's (my friend). It has a floor and it has kind of like windows. And it has a door. And it has kind of like a back window. I see pine straw and dirt and I used to see birds. Something happened to them. I see a lot of trees. I like the woods because I like to walk so much. I see a ditch in the woods. And sometimes I walk backwards on the short trail and the long trail. The End.

By January 1996, we were seeing great improvement in Eric's schoolwork, and Miss Scott was writing "very good" on several of his papers. A mid-period progress report in January showed that Eric was doing satisfactory work, completing all assignments and having good work habits and citizenship. Miss Scott wrote, "Eric is constantly improving."

Just as Eric was an observer in pre-school, he took on much the same role in kindergarten. It was a big deal for a student to get all smiley stickers on his behavior card each week, and Eric always did. However, for some of the students, that was a tough thing to accomplish. Miss Scott kept a small open folder for each student, and each day the students would start out with five colored strips. If the student misbehaved, a color strip was pulled. Eric knew each folder started out with the five colored strips for each student, so if someone had a color pulled, his chart was no longer complete. One day Eric noticed a couple of his fellow kindergarten classmates had colors missing, so he colored strips of paper, cut them out and put them in the folders. When Miss Scott discovered the "new" colors and found out Eric had helped his classmates out, she told us about it. We weren't sure if Eric didn't want his fellow

31

classmates to stay out of trouble, or if he was more concerned with every folder's being uniform.

Overall, Eric had a good year in kindergarten, and by the time school was out, he had been named Student of the Month (for December 1995), received a Super Eagle Award and had learned to read, add and subtract, among other skills. And he graduated from kindergarten.

The summer of 1996 provided an opportunity for Eric to participate in Safety Town, a five-day focus on several types of safety, such as safety in traffic and with strangers, sponsored by local law enforcement and several local businesses. It was held at A.C. Steere Elementary School in Shreveport and was open to students who had completed kindergarten. At that time, Eric had begun to be fascinated with traffic lights. He was thrilled with the first assignment on the first day, which was to correctly color a traffic light with red, green and yellow crayons. He didn't even bother to tell me goodbye when I was leaving. He sat down and got to work. The week was fun for him and a couple of his friends from kindergarten who rode together in a carpool. On the last day of the week of Safety Town, Eric received a diploma and got to shake hands with the police chief.

Chapter Five

Restaurants, Tails and First Grade

We enjoyed dining out occasionally, and we found that Eric loved to visit restaurants and "eat out." Of course, with just about all of the restaurants Eric visited at a young age, there was a prerequisite required: They had to have at least one ceiling fan.

One of Eric's favorite places to go was the Mexican restaurant, El Chico. He told me when he was very young, "I don't eat good at home. I eat better at El Chico."

When he was about five, we were at El Chico, and Eric ordered his own drink. Then he asked the waiter for a page that he could color and said his little brother needed one, too. That was a sweet gesture for Eric. However, his little brother was only a year old and probably would have tried to eat the crayon if he had been given the opportunity.

Another trip to a restaurant when he was a toddler resulted in Eric's not wanting to visit there again. The place was Chianti Restaurant, a very good Italian eatery. Eric was sitting in a high chair beside me one minute, and the next, he was on the floor. He must have leaned over too far and tipped the high chair over. Other diners came to our table to see about him as did the waiter. He cried a little but was fine a few minutes later. His memorable quote from that experience was "Don't want to go to Chianti. I want to go to Little Tiny Ino." Translated, Little Tiny Ino is L'Italiano, another Italian restaurant. At least he had the correct cuisine.

Eric's love for books was much like his fascination for ceiling fans. As noted earlier, he didn't merely watch the fan blades as they made their rotations, he also moved his hands, mimicking the movement of the blades. With books, he didn't only listen to the stories being read to him, he also put himself in them by acting them out. He went through a lengthy phase of enjoying books about Curious George, the cute little monkey adopted by the man who wore a yellow hat. He would act out Curious George and do some of the things in the books that the monkey did.

At about this same time, there were some obsessive-compulsive tendencies that were right under the surface. Eric was twirling again—his shirt tail, a string or whatever was available. He also walked on his toes and snapped his fingers a lot. The more people that were around, the more intense the manifestation and the more over-stimulated Eric would be. Also, there were times when Eric couldn't control his anger, particularly with his little brother. Dr. Horton, who always seemed to know what to do, prescribed time-out for Eric as a way to deal with the anger problem. She also slightly increased his dosage of Prozac to more effectively handle the obsessive-compulsive behavior. It was summertime, so that was the best time to alter Eric's medicine so that it wouldn't interfere with his schoolwork.

By the first of August, though, Eric was clearly over-medicated, and he was irritable, nervous, hyperactive and showing anxiety and impulsiveness. I didn't give him his Prozac that morning and called Dr. Horton, who told me to go back to his original dosage. Sometime during the summer of 1996, Dr. Horton had us leave off the Ritalin, so by August, Eric was taking only the small dose of Prozac. By the time school started for Eric's first-grade year, he was much better. He also was treating his little brother with more respect. One day Rob had taken the boys to McDonald's for lunch and to play in the indoor play park. Astonished, he watched from below to see Eric at the top of the slide with Kurt in his lap. Eric had his arms protectively around his little brother all the way down the slide. Tears came to Rob's eyes when he told me the story later that evening. That was a rare display of affection for Eric, but we were grateful it happened. The first time Eric had done something similar was several months earlier when Rob took the boys to the mall for a train ride. Eric and Kurt were the only passengers on the little train, but Rob put them in the same car and told Eric to take care of his little brother. Eric put his arm around Kurt and kept it there the whole time. For some reason, they were not enjoying the ride, and each time the train made its way around the circular track, their expressions were somber. It was not a joyful ride but a serious one. But Eric had taken care of Kurt, and that was the important thing.

Even though in the fall of 1996 Eric was better, he was experiencing occasional hyperactive outbreaks and a tendency to tear up certain things in his room. We found Eric did much better if he was involved in a project. He needed structure in his life. When he was lacking something to do, he would move around non-stop. We were happy to see Eric was finally able to sit still and watch a cartoon on television and be enraptured by it. After the cartoon was over, though, he would act out whatever he had watched. He would pretend to be a Doberman or the Road Runner. It was fascinating to watch him but worrisome because we didn't know how long the pretending would last. Would Eric always be like this? Would the pretending stop? Would he ever be like other kids his age?

During Eric's first-grade year, his teacher noticed a speech problem that she brought to our attention. We had him screened by the school's speech therapist, who found his articulation skills were fine and all sounds were made correctly. She did note that occasionally Eric lisped a bit on the "s" sound and that the cross-bite we noticed earlier was something we probably needed to have checked out with his dentist. Although Eric would not wear braces on his teeth until he was in the third grade, at least we were able to know something could be done about his cross-bite.

About this time in his life, Eric added one more thing to his list of obsessions—tails. Whenever he had to draw any type of mammal or large object, he would add a tail. George Washington got a tail. The Statue of Liberty got a tail. Eric was coloring in the lines now, but he added a tail to everything. This fascination would continue for several years. Eric began creating his own creatures to color and cut out, and each one had a tail. Adding the tails was odd, but Eric was becoming quite a good little artist. He made hundreds of these little creatures, all with vivid colors and bright expressions. It was hard to know just what was going through his mind, but he certainly had a lot of creativity and imagination.

With Eric, things were either black or white. There were no gray areas. He saw things as good or bad, right or wrong. He also took things literally. He had been visiting a neighborhood friend and playing in his yard when a hard rain began to fall. The friend's mom offered to drive Eric home, but he refused the ride and ran all the way home. She followed behind him in the car to make sure he made it safely and to tell me that she had offered to drive him home. I thanked her and told her he must have considered her a stranger. We had warned him about strangers and told him never get in a stranger's car.

At Eric's appointment with Dr. Horton in March 1997, I mentioned his fascination with tails and another rather strange activity that Eric had started--crawling around on the floor on all-fours. He wasn't just crawling, though. He could run very fast that way with his hands flat on the floor in front of his feet. He had started this after seeing "The Lion King," a popular animated movie at the time. We had taken a family trip to Tyler, Texas, to visit a zoo before Eric's little brother was born. After the visit to the zoo, we went to a park near downtown Tyler that had an outdoor amphitheater. Before we knew it, Eric was up on the stage, moving around, pointing and saying something. Rob and I moved closer to hear what he was saying, and we heard the words "the generations." We looked at each other, wondering where he got that and why he was talking about generations. Then I remembered. It was from "The Lion King." During a soliloquy, one of the characters talks about generations of time. Eric was mimicking the speech in the movie. This child had lived most of his life without an interest in cartoons and now not only was he interested in them, but also he was acting them out. He was living them, incorporating them into his life. In fact, by that time he was more interested in cartoons than he was in books. When I read to him, he was distracted. Sometimes I would have to ask Eric a question or tell him something as many as three times before getting a response.

There were a couple of obsessive-compulsive traits Eric was exhibiting. His P.E. teacher had mentioned Eric's walking on his toes, and he had a slight temptation to play with strings, but he was fairly easy to discourage. It was time to pull out the oven timer again that had worked well when he was in kindergarten. We would set the timer and tell Eric that he had two minutes or three minutes to play with strings and then he would have to put them away. Usually Eric would say, "I don't want to play with the strings now." He did not like the timer, and rather than have a set few minutes to play with them, he chose not do it at all.

Dr. Horton urged us to redirect Eric when he "got stuck" in obsessive behavior. If we could redirect him and it worked, the obsessive behavior would not get in the way of Eric's activities.

The first few months of first grade were good for Eric. He made all "A's" on his report card for the first nine weeks, he held the prestigious honor of Student of the Month for his classroom for the month of September, and he won Best Halloween Costume in his class. Eric was a Dalmatian for Halloween and wore a costume that Rob and I made. It wasn't elaborate and was made out of white sweatpants and a white turtleneck shirt with black magic marker dots all over both the pants and shirt. Rob made ears out of a piece of black felt cloth and sewed them onto a baseball cap. The crowning touch was a black magic marker dot on the tip of Eric's nose. But the most important thing, at least to Eric, was the long black tail that we attached on the back of the sweatpants. Eric didn't care what he was supposed to be for Halloween, as long as he had a tail.

The first-grader seemed to be focused and was progressing along as expected. Always hopeful that Eric would be able to function without medication, we discussed with Dr. Horton whether to try to wean him off the Prozac. We decided to try it during the Christmas holidays. There was no noticeable change at first, and we were encouraged that he would be able to leave off the medication after having been on it for more than a year.

As winter turned into spring and plants and flowers began their yearly transformation, Eric was changing, too. He was becoming anxious and afraid, and his mind was getting "stuck" on depressing thoughts. His whole life changed, probably gradually but it seemed to take a downward turn overnight. He began to cry at school and not want to attend. We never allowed him to stay home during this time, but it was very hard to put him on the bus in the mornings.

In mid-April, there was a bad storm that hit our area, and a large pine tree in our neighbor's back yard was uprooted and crashed into another tree. As a result, our power was knocked out. The thunder scared Eric so much that he began to call the incident "the big boom day."

One morning, Eric's teacher, Shelley Lowery, called me and reported that Eric was upset and crying, thinking he was hearing thunder. He had cried the afternoon before for the same reason. Eric had been asking a lot of questions about thunder and lightning after the storm. I contacted Dr. Horton, who said Eric's crying spells were either caused by excessive fearfulness about storms or he was hearing noises. She told me to discontinue his Ritalin dose that she had started Eric back on so we could determine if he was having auditory hallucinations that were medicine-induced. "If the crying continues," she said, "we'll evaluate it further." Even though the storm had happened several days before, Eric was obsessing about the incident that made him fearful, and this was a delayed stress reaction. We ended our telephone conversation with Dr. Horton's saying to call her in three days and report on Eric's progress. I called Dr. Horton back on Friday, April 21, reporting that Eric was still afraid he was going to hear thunder and was holding his ears. I made a journal entry in the form of notes for Dr. Horton. I wrote:

We've held off on the Ritalin. Eric doesn't seem to be affected by not taking it. Today he's been crying about school, saying he's not wanting to go because he's tired of school.

We read three books on thunder and lightning and although he's obsessing about it, he doesn't seem to have that on his mind as much as he does just not wanting to go to school.

He told me some second graders were picking on him, but when questioned further, he said it happened at the first of the year.

Then he said in the afternoons the class has to sit for a long time on the floor while Mrs. Lowery, his teacher, reads to them. 'It takes a long time to get back to my chair,' Eric said.

I don't know what to do if he cries tomorrow morning about not wanting to go.

He's not eaten well this weekend. He thought he was going to get another week off after Easter.

Dr. Horton told me if Eric is frightened, he's afraid he's not safe. "Let him know he's safe at school," she said. As far as his appetite, she said to offer him foods he likes that are high in protein, such as peanut butter and cheese. She instructed me to hold the Ritalin dosage and start Eric back on the Prozac.

On April 23, 1997, Mrs. Lowery wrote:

Mrs. Vardeman,

Eric still cried most of the day today. He said he was tired of school. He wanted to call you, but I told him school would be over soon. I felt really bad for him, but I didn't want him to think he would be able to call home every day. I hope that was okay.

He isn't disturbing the class and he's still getting all of his work done.

Please let me know if there is anything I need to do.

Thanks,

Shelley Lowery

On April 25 at 1 p.m., Mrs. Lowery wrote that Eric had a "pretty good day. He didn't cry at all until after lunch when it started raining. Big improvement from yesterday." She noted at

1:40 p.m. that the loud thunder really scared him. "I held his hand and he got okay."

Three days later, another note from Mrs. Lowery said: "This morning Eric cried quite a bit. This afternoon was much better. He hardly cried at all. He said, 'I'm very ready for Spring Break. I need it'."

I reported to Dr. Horton on April 30 by phone. Eric was still saying he was tired of going to school and was scared of thunder and noises in general. She recommended continuing the Prozac until his "phobic avoidance to school passes. Even when he's on an even keel, he's an anxious little boy."

Eric's schoolwork began to suffer that spring, also. His weekly progress reports went from all "A's" and "B's" to "B's" and "C's" and an occasional "D." Even though he was having all of these problems, he managed to bring his grades up to all "A's" and "B's" on his report card and missed only seven days of school all year in the first grade. During the stressful month of April, Eric tested for Discoveries, a program for students who teachers thought could handle a challenge. The Discoveries students were able to spend some time out of the regular classroom and do science experiments and other educational studies. Eric didn't make it into the program, but I wonder if he had been tested before April whether the results would have been different.

During that difficult period in his life, Eric also began obsessing that something was going to happen to me. He was afraid I was going to die. There was nothing I could tell him or that anyone else could say to convince him that his mom was healthy, everything was going to be all right, and he didn't need to worry. Dr. Horton said he was experiencing separation anxiety. We talked about sending Eric to school for three or four days in the mornings only and checking him out at noon. We never did that, but it was considered during this time because he was in such a low state. Although Eric never minded going to see Dr. Horton, he had never been too eager to go, mainly because he didn't like to have to sit in the waiting room. I knew he must be feeling low because he asked me if we could go see Dr. Horton. "I feel tired inside," he said.

Dr. Horton's explanation of separation anxiety made sense. "The problem now is anxiety about school. He has obsessive thinking and then he becomes afraid. The medicine is helpful, but he needs to be assured in school." Some children experience separation anxiety after they've been out of school when they are ill or have been on vacation and have to go back to school, she explained. They have a "school phobia," and they have difficulty because they don't want to be away from their parents.

Play therapy was suggested by Dr. Horton, a time that would give Eric a distracting activity and serve as a medium of expression. "He can communicate his fears, and they will become less threatening." Also, we were to try hard to distract Eric from the anxiety, continue to reassure him his job was to go to school and "mom would take care of mom." Giving Eric a reward for staying in school each day also was suggested. "It only reinforces the problem if you take him out of school," Dr. Horton said. If Eric told us he was tired of school, we were to tell him, "I know you are and I'm sorry."

I had written some of Eric's comments that week: "It's rough at school. There have been long days at school. I'm just tired of going a long time. I like to watch TV at home. It takes a long time to come home from school. I don't like being away from mama." The last statement was baffling to me because he never had called me "mama." I was Mother.

In addition to being worried about Eric, I felt sorry for Mrs. Lowery, his teacher. She did the best she could in trying to help Eric make it through each day. I knew, in addition to Eric, she had 22 other students to teach. She did an outstanding job of giving Eric the help he needed while tending to the needs of the other students. Eric liked Mrs. Lowery and probably had a little crush on her. She was young and pretty with olive skin and long, dark hair. "Mrs. Lowery has red lips," Eric said, one day shortly after school started.

Nevertheless, during one of his low points, Eric became so upset, he threw up at school. He also had started losing weight and was beginning to look too thin. He was slim before he started having anxiety problems, so he certainly did not need to lose any weight. Dr. Horton monitored his weight at each visit and always asked about his appetite. It wasn't good during this time, and we tried to prepare foods he liked or visit his favorite restaurants to encourage him to eat.

After church one Sunday, we invited a young church friend to Mr. Gatti's to eat pizza with us. For a while having someone else along helped to get Eric's mind off being afraid, but halfway to the restaurant, during the meal and all the way home, Eric started verbalizing his anxiety. There was nothing we could say to keep him from worrying.

I've never experienced depression myself, but I've read enough about it to know it is not something a person can talk himself out of. It is a disease that needs medication, counseling and a lot of prayer. Even our little six-year-old knew he needed prayer. One day Eric asked me if we could pray that he would not feel so sad. We prayed, and then I went to Rob, sobbing as I told him what Eric had requested. He so badly wanted to feel better and not be sad and afraid.

A family friend whom I had worked for in her office of Christian ministry offered to pray for Eric. I took Eric to the Rev. Frances Attaway, an ordained minister and author, who placed her hands on Eric and had me do the same. She prayed a genuine, inspired prayer over Eric that lifted the spirits of both Eric and me. I could feel the presence of God surrounding us and filling us with comfort and relief from the stress that had been consuming our lives.

Eric's bout of anxiety/depression had affected our entire family and is one of the hardest things we've ever lived through. At some point after things began to get bad for Eric, we saw Dr. Horton. She looked at me and noticed some weight loss. "You've got to get yourself together," she said. We all had the blues and were having a hard time dealing with Eric's anxiety and depression. It had even affected Kurt, who at only two years old, was moping around the house like the rest of us. Dr. Horton put Eric back on his dosage of Prozac, but it took awhile before the medicine got into his system and we could see some improvement in his moods. Those were some difficult days that our family would not want to re-live.

Chapter Six

Another Added Worry

At our visit to Dr. Horton in June, I reported Eric had a destructive nature and was doing some things without thinking, such as stepping into the small swimming pool in the back yard to get something while still having shoes and socks on his feet. His constant eye blinking was a problem, too. Dr. Horton talked about Tourette Syndrome, a disorder of the nervous system characterized by unwanted movements and noises, or tics. Named after a French physician, Georges Gille de la Tourette, Tourette Syndrome is defined by Merriam-Webster's Dictionary as "a rare disease characterized by involuntary tics and by uncontrollable verbalization involving esp. echolalia and the use of obscene language." Echolalia is the "often pathological repetition of what is said by other people as if echoing them," according to Merriam-Webster's.

I personally did not know anyone who had Tourette Syndrome but had heard of it and was taken aback by Dr. Horton's mention of the disorder. Although I was saddened to realize that Eric had OCD and ADHD, I had gotten used to the idea and was learning to live with the realization. I just didn't think I could bear his having another "syndrome."

Dr. Horton said the eye blinking seemed to be a tic as was the nose twitching she was observing Eric to have. I questioned whether Prozac could cause the tics, and she said the drug was not known to cause twitches and tics. Nonetheless, she wanted us to suspend the Prozac to see if the eye blinking and nose twitching would go away and to use a humidifier in Eric's room at night. Stress causes the tics to be worse, so we were going to do whatever we could to keep the stress level down.

In June we took a vacation to Destin, Florida, with Rob's parents, and Eric and Kurt had a great time playing in the gulf and on the sand at the beach. We had our hands full trying to lather our blond-haired, fair-skinned boys with sunscreen. They didn't spend much time indoors and loved being in the water.

We saw Dr. Horton on August 16, and I reported that Eric had been physically active during the summer. However, his concentration was lacking when we read together. "He doesn't have the power to concentrate," I had written in my notes. "If I'm reading to Eric, he asks questions not related to the book. He's not following along in the hymnal in church. He's not focusing with his mind."

We had left off the Ritalin during the summer, and Dr. Horton told us to start Eric back on the medication. She also told me to "get calories into him." He weighed 48 ¾ pounds and was getting taller, so he really looked thin.

I asked Dr. Horton if she was familiar with a book that was published in 1996 by Dr. Jeffrey M. Schwartz titled *Brain Lock,* a four-step method that recommends using behavior therapy to treat OCD. The method uses the concept of self-treatment to overcome the urges to do compulsive behaviors and learn ways to cope with obsessive thoughts. She was familiar with the book and agreed that behavior therapy works well, but if OCD is treated with both behavior therapy and medication, the best result is achieved.

In addition to the lack of concentration, Eric was having some anger problems. Dr. Horton said to let him know that his behavior comes with a consequence, and the consequence should be immediate, intense and for a short duration (one minute for each year of his life). "He needs to let his anger out," she said, "but he needs to know it's not ok to behave that way when he's angry." Dr. Horton also mentioned another punishment we could try: an early bedtime of 15 or 20 minutes for bad behavior.

School started for Eric's second-grade year on August 25. Almost immediately, he had problems concentrating and seemed confused on what he needed to do and what homework was assigned. Eric's teacher, Fern Brimmer, had to take four weeks off for medical reasons beginning the second week of school, and I kept in contact with the substitute teacher. The sub reported there seemed to be a difference in Eric's concentration from the morning to the afternoon. He was taking the Ritalin in the mornings only, so after reporting this information to Dr. Horton, she increased his dosage to help him be able to concentrate. Shortly after that, he was able to focus better and his grades improved almost immediately.

During this second-grade year, Eric developed a bad habit of rushing through his classwork and marking answers to questions almost at random. We could never put our finger on why he was doing this. Several times during the year, Mrs. Brimmer would send a math worksheet or reading assignment with questions home with Eric so he could redo the papers correctly. On one of the papers titled "What do you need...," the assignment was to match pictures with descriptions. For example, there was a picture of a typewriter which should have been matched to "1. What do you need to write a newspaper story?" Eric put letters in the boxes containing the pictures when he should have put numbers. Mrs. Brimmer wrote, "Please help Eric do this over—Don't know where he got letters instead of numbers for the boxes." Eric would complain when he had to do the sheets over at home. We tried to remind him that his "job" was to go to school and do the best he could on everything he was assigned and then he wouldn't have to do the work over at home. For some reason, that didn't register with him or something else was going on that we didn't discover.

Even though he was rushing through some assignments, Eric's writing showed a lot of imagination, and he liked to write about animals and draw them, probably because he liked to draw tails. A writing and drawing assignment from Friday, October 17, 1997, although brief, got right to the point:

This is my cat, my cat gits in to a lot of trubul. And he ran out side and a dog ran after the cat.

Another paper from November was titled "When I Grow Up...," and the assignment was to draw a picture of what you might look like when you grow up and write what you want to be and why. Eric drew a big smiley face in the circle on the page and then filled in the blank with the word, "doctor," but he spelled it, "doctrer." Then he wrote:

I take good care of chirdrin. And I give them a shot. And they have to stay there. And then they can go home. And if they have to come back agane they will have to get another shot.

I'm sure Eric was like most other children who thought about shots when they had to visit the pediatrician rather than the lollipop they were given when the visit was over. That was one great thing noted by Eric about visiting Dr. Horton: She didn't give shots, so Eric never minded going to see her.

One writing assignment Eric completed in second grade was to make a small illustrated booklet called "I Am Happy." Eric's "happy" booklet involved animals and Christmas:

First page: *Today we or going to the cocus (circus) and I am happy.*

Second page: *We or at the cocus now.*

Third page: *And a dog was thar. And wen it was time to go home I criyd.*

Fourth page: *And my dad put me to bed.*

Fifth page: *And the next morning I ate brefust, and went to school.*

Sixth page: *And wen I got home it was Christmas. And I was happy.*

It was during the second grade we noticed Eric had trouble understanding what he was reading. It was evident with his answers on a problem-solving math sheet. The assignment was to circle the correct answer and write the answer in a sentence. The first problem was:

Jake collects coins. He has 197 pennies. How many will Jake have if he gets 3 more?

The sheet gave a choice between 197 + 3 = _____ and 197 − 3 = _____. Eric wrote "200" in each blank and then for the sentence, he wrote: *Jake collects 3 coins.*

The next problem:

Jake has a book of silver dollars. The book has 5 pages. There are 4 silver dollars on each page. How many silver dollars are in the book?

The choice was 5 + 4 = _____ or 5 x 4 = _____. Eric wrote "9" and "20," respectively, and for his sentence, he wrote: *Jake has 5 pages.*

When Eric tried, he could do math problems because when we asked him questions, he could answer them. His problem was in reading, understanding what he read and following directions.

There were some things Eric was either too busy to correct or didn't bother to correct. He had trouble remembering to indent when he was writing paragraphs. Everything was either flush left to the margin, or if he indented, each line was indented and lined up one under the other. Maybe Eric thought it looked out of balance if only the first line was indented. Nonetheless, he wrote some interesting stories. He must have wanted wings. For several days, in his writing journal, he wrote of flying. From Wednesday, October 8, 1997:

> *I dreamed of flying day and night. And I flew in a cloud. I flew higher and higher and the next morning I woke up and I was in another country. And that country was in Mexico and I was happy. The End.*

From Wednesday, November 5, 1997:

> *Eric dreamed of flying day and night. I dreamed of my school too. I dreamed of a color and it was red and I wanted to go back home. But I could not go home. One day I was in a farm and there were cows and bulls too.*

We had visited Bayou Pierre Alligator Park near Natchitoches, Louisiana, during the summer, and Eric loved seeing the 'gators in the swampy water. He and his brother got to hold a baby alligator, whose mouth was taped shut, and have their picture made. In the photo, Eric, cradling the alligator in his arms, has a huge grin on his face, while his brother is sitting some distance away, not touching the alligator and not exactly smiling. Eric probably fondly remembered the visit when he wrote a fictional story about alligators and some policemen who made many futile attempts to remove some alligators from a river in a neighborhood and deposit them in another river. After getting bitten several times by the alligators in their attempts to control the reptiles, the police ended up having to shoot them. I guess Eric couldn't figure out a way to have the police and the alligators all live happily ever after.

We saw Dr. Horton on January 17, 1998, and discussed some problems Eric was having socially, particularly that he was not interacting with other children. Eric wanted to do his own thing and wasn't concerned with rules or proper etiquette. For this reason, other children found it hard to play with him, and he was being shunned by his classmates. Dr. Horton suggested engaging Eric in games with other children at home where he could practice taking turns. Some of the games she suggested were Uno and Toss Across, the latter which also would help Eric with motor skills. Juggling was also mentioned to help with motor skills but not until he reached age 10 or so. Dr. Horton noticed some "lispy noise" and told us to report any oddities in language that we noticed. Eric's current obsession was Wile E. Coyote, the cartoon coyote who although always unsuccessful, never gave up pursuit of the speedy Road Runner.

We welcomed a new member of the family that spring—Lucy—a five-week-old black and white Fox Terrier with an underbite. Lucy was a birthday gift for Eric and Kurt, who were turning eight and four, respectively. The first thing Eric did when we got Lucy home was sprint into the house, retrieve a sketch pad and pencil and attempt to draw a picture of Lucy. The little dog was very excited about being in a new place and ran around non-stop. Eric ran around, too, following Lucy and getting a bit frustrated because the puppy wouldn't be still and pose for her picture to be drawn.

For some reason, April seemed to be a difficult month for Eric. Just as he had some problems with anxiety and depression during the month of April in first grade, Eric began to have some issues in second grade during that month. I received a note from Mrs. Brimmer on April 2, 1998:

Would you be able to meet with me at 7:45 tomorrow a.m.? I know it's short

notice, but if not, we'll try to plan a time next week. Seems like Eric is making some changes I'd like to discuss with you.

Thanks,

Fern Brimmer

I met with Mrs. Brimmer the next day. She was concerned that Eric's work was messy, he was giving off-the-wall answers to oral questions, and on the written ones, he was displaying a lack of awareness. Eric was not aware of certain things that he should have been noticing, such as his pencil needing sharpening and sloppy handwriting. He was trying to hurry and get through with his work and on many occasions, he's "tuned us out," Mrs. Brimmer said. I called Dr. Horton, and she adjusted his medication. A few days later, Mrs. Brimmer wrote again:

Eric seems to be a little more aware though I haven't noticed a big change. He asked to sharpen his pencil – I usually have to tell him when it needs sharpening. Also, I believe his writing is a little neater. He's writing on the lines and isn't writing letters on top of letters.

Thank you,

Fern Brimmer

Later that same week, Mrs. Brimmer was reporting Eric seemed to be more aware and had answered an oral question immediately and correctly. That was one problem that was solved, but the pencil sharpening incident was another example of how things that came naturally for most children did not come naturally for Eric. Did he realize his pencil needed sharpening and eventually would not write at all unless it was sharpened? Did he care?

We had a Dr. Horton appointment on April 25, and she wanted us to continue Eric's current medication dosage. She noted that Eric was walking on his toes at the clinic, and we reported that he was doing that some at home. Although we did not discuss Eric's toe-walking with Dr. Horton, we learned later it is a common trait among persons with autism. When Eric talked with Dr. Horton without Rob and me in the room, he told her he didn't have anything worrying him at the time. Then he said, "It will be nice if it rains to wash away the pollen." He was probably having some allergy trouble, something unfortunately Eric inherited from both of his parents.

On April 28, Rob's mom and I attended a workshop on ADD at Lakeview United Methodist Church in Shreveport. One of the speakers was Dr. Marci Howard with the Counseling Center Network. Some of the information Dr. Howard spoke about regarding ADD and ADHD in children, I was fairly aware of, but it was interesting to hear the characteristics of each described in this way. An ADHD child is unable to focus, his brain is always firing and he is unable to concentrate, she said. Also, he is hyperactive and lacks short-term memory. I was thinking about how correctly this behavior described Eric. The ADD child is the opposite in behavior and is sluggish. Either child can't help how his brain is processing the information, but behavior modification works well with both types of problems, Dr. Howard explained. The child can learn how to modify things and live with his disorder. She also talked about the use of an Acuscope that was developed in Germany by scientists to produce cell activity that worked as a mood elevator. If medication isn't doing enough for the child, the Acuscope can help children with ADD and ADHD in aiding their short-term memory and organizational skills, she said. Ear clips are placed on each ear and an electrical current goes from one side to another, relaxing the child and allowing his brain to go into the alpha state, when the brain is in a relaxed but aware state. Years later I would hear more about the Acuscope and its uses in pain management and have it used even on myself to treat temporomandibular joint disorder (TMJ) and its accompanying jaw pain. We never had the Acuscope used on Eric, but it was very interesting to learn about it at the workshop.

In addition to learning more about ADD and ADHD, I gained something else from the workshop. Another speaker there was Cindy Batten, a certified school psychologist, who talked about Section 504 and the Rehabilitation Action of 1973. This was the first time I had heard of the law that prohibits the discriminatory assignment of disabled students to segregated classes and mandates that certain modifications be made for students who qualify. I knew that Eric did not need to be separated from other students in his regular classroom, but I was interested in finding out more about Section 504.

Even though Eric's grades were good with "A's," "B's" and "C's," he still was having to redo much of his class work at home. We had received the results of his Iowa Test of Basic Skills, and the results showed that Eric scored low in several key areas including vocabulary, reading comprehension, language development, math problem solving and thinking skills. The only area that Eric scored high in was health and safety. Rob and I started thinking that Eric might need to be held back and repeat second grade. There were several concepts we didn't feel that he had grasped, particularly if the Iowa Test was accurate, and we were concerned that he would be too far behind to catch up if he went on to third grade. Another possibility we discussed was having Eric tutored during the summer to try to catch him up to where he needed to be. Time was running out, though, because it was May and school would be out in a few weeks.

We talked to Mrs. Brimmer on May 6 about our thoughts on holding Eric back, and she was surprised that we were considering it. She said she believed there was nothing wrong with Eric intellectually but that processing was the problem. As an example, she said his picture interpretation is "way off." In a classroom assignment, the question was which sense was used to taste, and Eric marked the nose. Another question was what happens when water loses a lot of heat, and Eric marked a soft drink can. I told her that we felt in addition to Eric's not having grasped certain skills, we believed he was socially immature. I mentioned Section 504 and that we were interested in having Eric tested.

Three days after the meeting with Mrs. Brimmer, we had an appointment with Dr. Horton and reported that he was still giving off-the-wall answers to questions and that his teacher believed the problem was in the way Eric processed things. We told her that we were pursuing having Eric evaluated to see if he qualified under Section 504. We also mentioned we were considering pushing for Eric to repeat the second grade. I asked Dr. Horton if she believed holding him back would hurt him emotionally more than help him academically. She said we needed to take the lead from the teachers and school because they would be the best sources to tell us if he needed retention. Dr. Horton suggested retention only if the teachers pushed for it. It would not benefit Eric to hold him back because it would not help him to mature to be around children who were less mature than he was. Then she mentioned something neither Rob nor I had ever heard of—Asperger's Syndrome.

Chapter Seven

Asperger's Syndrome, "Little Professors" and Lots of Tests

Dr. Horton's mention of the words "Asperger's Syndrome" made me shiver. What could this be? We already had worried that he might have Tourette Syndrome. Now something else? I was not sure I could handle this.

In her gentle, informative way, Dr. Horton explained that Eric was intelligent but had a "very narrow range of interests" and he was behind developmentally in both social and motor skills. These are characteristics of Asperger's Syndrome, a form of autism, she said, explaining that Asperger's is a pervasive developmental disorder (PDD), a disorder characterized by delayed development of social and communication skills. There are many symptoms of PDD, but some include problems using and understanding language, difficulty relating to people, repetitive body movements or behaviors and unusual play with toys, according to the National Institute of Neurological Disorders and Stroke. *That explains a lot*, I thought, as I remembered Eric's strange use of toys. He never really played with them, at least not like other kids and not how they were designed to be used.

Children with Asperger's are like "little professors," Dr. Horton explained, because they know a lot about certain subjects. That was certainly true about Eric and how he had lived his life focusing on one field of interest at a time—ceiling fans, music and animals with tails.

After we got home, we began researching Asperger's Syndrome to find out everything we could about this disorder that was now used to describe our young son. At least we had a specific name for his condition, and we could begin to focus on how to improve on helping him. The term "little professors" was what Hans Asperger, who discovered Asperger's Syndrome, used to describe his patients. Asperger, a native of Vienna who studied the patterns of certain boys, discovered their similar traits of lack of empathy, little ability to form friendships, one-sided conversation, intense absorption in a special interest and clumsy movement.

We knew from Dr. Horton that Asperger's was under the umbrella of autism, and Rob and I began to talk about similarities between Eric and Raymond Babbitt, the Dustin Hoffman character in the 1988 movie "Rain Man." Raymond is an autistic savant who is so impaired by his autism that he lives in an institution. He also lives in a world of his own and is extremely lacking in social skills. But he can memorize anything; his brain functions as a calculator and processes math in an unbelievable fashion. He needs to have certain things in place in his room and in his life. He eats cheese balls with a toothpick, and the syrup must be on the table before his pancakes. He keeps impeccable notes in notebooks and knows seemingly thousands of facts about baseball. Even though Raymond's is an extreme case, there are some similar traits between Eric and the Rain Man, particularly in the rigidness of life and in specialized interest in certain subjects.

As we worked toward having Eric tested for Section 504 and meeting with teachers, counselors and Blanchard Elementary Principal Jan Becken, we discovered there were not enough school days left in the year for the process to be completed. We decided to pursue having Eric tested the next year, to let him advance to third grade and to have him tutored during the summer. We also filled out a form for Eric to attend summer school at North Highlands Elementary School, but we decided not to submit it after deciding to have him tutored. We also weren't sure he was qualified to attend summer school if he wasn't being retained.

In addition to the school system's evaluation and testing for Section 504, Dr. Horton said she wanted Eric to undergo more extensive diagnostic testing at the LSU Children's Center. This testing would need to come later after he got a little older. Rob and I were happy that the various tests would take place. The more tests performed on Eric, the more we could learn about him and the more we and others could do for him.

Eric had a tutor for the summer, Beverly Nichols, who worked with him on math and reading concepts. Mrs. Nichols taught him using a reading strategy known as SQ2R (Survey, Question, Read and Review) to help Eric with reading comprehension. She told him to look for key words in story problems for math, such as how many *in all* (add), how many are there *all together* (add), how many *more* (subtract) and how many *were left* (subtract). The tutor worked with him one or two days each week, and he seemed to do well having one-on-one help.

The summer of 1998 was a busy one for Eric. He had tutoring, was taking gymnastics, went to Vacation Bible School at our church, had a vacation in Gulf Shores, Alabama, with our family and his grandparents, and was scheduled to take swimming lessons in August.

On July 18, we had an appointment with Dr. Horton, and I reported that the tutor was working with Eric and had commented that the information is "there in his brain; he just has trouble knowing where to go to retrieve it." The tutor said he doesn't have a short-term memory problem, just a retrieving problem.

We also conveyed a concern to Dr. Horton about a noise Eric was making when he was idle or his mind was not focused. "He makes it continually. The only time he's not doing it is when he's in deep concentration," I had written in my notes. "He says he can't help it." He was making the noise in Vacation Bible School along with blinking his eyes a lot. The tutor also noticed the noise when she was working with him. On the day of our appointment, Dr. Horton noted Eric's facial grimaces and mouth twitching and that he was "very active" at the clinic.

Eric seemed nervous, anxious and agitated. When we were in Gulf Shores on vacation in June, Rob's dad had tripped and fallen in a restaurant. Eric showed great concern about his grandfather and even sat in his lap at the table later that evening. Any time Mr. Vardeman got up to walk across the floor, Eric was glued to him and telling him to be careful. Another example of Eric's anxiety was his worry about our dog, Lucy. He couldn't sit still to eat and kept getting up to check on the dog, afraid she would get out of the fenced-in back yard. Eric had spent a lot of time in "time out" because of hitting or kicking his little brother. "When Kurt walks by, Eric usually does it (hits or kicks him) automatically," I had written.

Dr. Horton told us to stop the Ritalin to see if the tics would go away. While the drug works well for attention and focusing problems, it can cause excessive hyperactivity, Dr. Horton said. She also wanted us to slightly increase Eric's Prozac dosage. He was now eight years old, weighed more and had probably outgrown the initial dosage. As always with a change in Eric's medication, Dr. Horton told us to watch for problems such as sleep disturbance, appetite loss or becoming jittery.

When school started for Eric's third-grade year, I quickly scheduled a parent-teacher conference to visit with his teacher, Teresa Taylor, fill her in on Eric's situation and convey that we were anxious to get Eric's testing done for Section 504. I told her to please let me know if she noticed any changes in Eric's behavior or schoolwork. She said some of the teachers had told her about his prior problems but that so far she wasn't seeing any.

We saw Dr. Horton two months later, on September 19, and found that Eric had gained one and a half pounds from July. He was going to have a dentist appointment the next month to have four baby teeth pulled in preparation for braces, and I wanted to know whether we should leave off his medication because he was going to have to take Demerol and Vistaril because of a bad gag reflex. Dr. Horton told us to leave off his regular medication, noting that one day of not taking the Prozac dosage would not hurt because the drug still would be in his body.

We reported that so far Eric was settling in fine in third grade, his teacher was not seeing any problems and his grades were good. We felt that his self-confidence level was up, in part because of tutoring and gymnastics. He was walking and running more correctly by putting weight on his heels instead of his toes.

A concern we reported to Dr. Horton was that Eric was not picking up on the emotional states of people around him. It didn't come naturally to him to realize when someone was upset or angry. "A deficit (of Asperger's Syndrome) is feeling. It's hard for him to understand the feeling states of one person or another," Dr. Horton said. She suggested that we talk with Eric's teacher, letting her know that Eric had difficulty in understanding emotional states. Also, we were to talk with Eric and encourage his "social memory" to recall things about interaction with people. "Happy is the easiest emotion (to understand). Anything that feels good, they equate happy with," she said. We were to start with the family first and then work outside the family. If Eric got mad at his little brother, we were to ask Eric how he was feeling when he became angry. If Kurt was in a bad mood, we were to ask Eric why he thought Kurt was feeling that way. Letting the brothers work out their own differences and arguments when possible was something we could do that would help them both mature.

At that same appointment, Dr. Horton noted that Eric was "pacing in circles here" and doing a lot of writing in a notebook he brought with him.

It was October before Eric's screening for dyslexia began, but it was done in two parts, the second half's being in November. He was also scheduled for speech and language screening. I wanted to make sure Eric knew what would be happening and when it would happen so that he wouldn't be rattled about being taken out of class. I found if I prepared Eric for something out of the ordinary, he would be more relaxed about having to do it. In the meantime, the first nine weeks' report card came out, and for the first time in his life, Eric had a "D" and an "F." The "D" was in health and the "F" was in science. Most of the science grade was made up of having to copy items from the blackboard onto notebook paper. Eric could not grasp the concept for some reason. I was getting frustrated because of the time wasted on waiting for the testing to be completed. That was time that could be spent on getting Eric some help. I realized it was not the fault of the school. There was a lot of paperwork involved with the school board, and

I'm sure other students throughout the parish were on the list to be tested as well.

I wrote Eric's teacher, Mrs. Taylor, a note expressing my concerns about his grades and about the time it was taking to get the testing process completed. "We haven't told Eric about his report card for fear that it will damage his self-esteem," I wrote. "He truly loves school, and if he loses that feeling or feels he is a failure, I'm afraid he might dread going or even give up. He would be devastated. I know he's trying, and if his attention is still good, it must be the processing problem causing him to make the bad grades."

In the midst of my anxiety over waiting for the report, Eric gave me a sweet note that he had written for me:

November 14, 1998

Dear Mom I love you. You are my best friend I ever had.

After reading the note, I felt I could handle anything. I think it was Eric's way of saying "thank you" for being his mom. I am so thankful I've been given the opportunity.

When the dyslexia report was completed, it was enlightening but not completely surprising, in that we had expected some of the results. Carolyn Gardner, a reading specialist with Caddo Parish, had performed the screening, and she wrote:

Eric appeared to want to perform well during the assessment, and he seemed to enjoy listening for sounds. His teacher reported that Eric's performance is inconsistent in the classroom and that he tends to do poorly when he has not been told what to expect.

Eric was given a battery of tests that formed the basis of the dyslexia report: The Criterion Referenced Spelling Test (CRST), the Primary Reading Skills test, the Slosson Oral Reading Test-Revised (SORT-R), the Diagnostic Reading Scales (DRS) and the Comprehensive Receptive and Expressive Vocabulary Test

(CREVT). His Iowa Test of Basic Skills scores also were included in the report. (Complete results of Eric's dyslexia testing are listed in the Appendix at the back of this book).

Eric's scores on the tests were varied. He scored 94% on the CRST, a written language exam, spelling correctly 30 of the 33 words, correctly spelling a dictated sentence and writing a simplistic story in a three-minute time frame. He wrote:

I like to play ball sometimes, and I like to play chace (chase). Some times I like to play with my friends. And I like to play with my dog. And I like to play with my brother.

Mrs. Gardner wrote in her report: "The writing sample was written with simplistic language, with every sentence containing 'I like to play...' and no elaboration of what games he plays with his friends or his brother."

His scores on the Primary Reading Skills test, a test to check coding skills, ranged from 80% to 100% and covered consonants, vowels and syllables.

Eric's reading comprehension was measured by the SORT-R and the DRS, and he scored at the beginning of the fourth grade on the SORT-R but scored poorly on the DRS, correctly answering only four out of eight questions on one 3.5 grade-level passage and only one out of eight on another.

An oral language test, the CREVT was the toughest test of all for Eric. He scored in the 3rd percentile for receptive and 30th percentile for expressive, with a total of 7th percentile (poor range).

Eric's Iowa Test scores from second grade were made a part of the report and ranged from 4th percentile in reading and science to 31st percentile in listening.

In her recommendations, Mrs. Gardner wrote that the CREVT score indicates that Eric might have difficulty understanding grade-level material, even though his expressive vocabulary was average. Due to the low score on the CREVT, she administered the Kaufman Brief Test of Intelligence which indicated "functioning to be in the low average range." Eric's grades have mostly been "A's" and "B's" with one "C" in reading in the second grade; however, the Iowa Test scores were lower than would be expected of a child with those grades, she wrote. "The SORT-R and DRS indicate Eric can read words slightly above grade level, but the comprehension scores are below grade level." She noted the days of the week and the months of the year were written quickly, "perhaps because they involve rote memory. However, the writing sample must include creative ideas, and it took much longer for Eric to write."

The remainder of her report is as follows:

Eric's performance on academic tasks is inconsistent. It appears that he does well when he has had the opportunity to memorize, such as writing the days and months or performing math calculations. However, when he must apply the knowledge of math calculations to problems, answer comprehension questions about a story or write an original story, he has difficulty.

It is recommended that Eric be given an opportunity to relate new situations to previously solved problems as much as possible. For example, when a new math problem is encountered, he should be guided in comparing it to a similar problem he has solved before. He should be taught to look for key facts in science and social studies paragraphs (Project Read Report Form) and to focus on the happenings (events) in narrative stories (Project Read Story Form). He may need extended time to complete tasks so he can organize the components into categories to compare to previously known material. He should be praised when he attempts tasks that appear new to him. His progress should be monitored closely to determine if he needs more intensive accommodations and modifications.

I met with Mrs. Gardner on November 18, and she reviewed Eric's test results with me. To help Eric with reading comprehension in context subjects such as science and social studies, she suggested he look for the important thing in each sentence, or, in other words, pick out the key fact. With narrative stories, he should look for the goal of the main character or what keeps the character from solving the problem in the story. She suggested underlining key words in sentences. She told me Eric memorizes well, which I had known already, but Eric needed to form some coping skills because each year the material would get harder, and he "can't always have it in perfect order." The major thing to do at home, she said, is to help Eric make connections from one situation to another and point out what is similar in both and verbalize this with him. I was grateful for the suggestions and vowed to do my best to help Eric.

The most important thing that happened as a result of having Eric screened was now he could have the accommodations he needed to help him in school. It was at this point he received preferential seating at the front of the classroom, extended time on tests and occasionally had questions read to him orally. Eric's specific accommodation plan listed the following: Extended time limits/response time, Simplified/repeated directions, Reduced written work, Repeated review/drill, Slower pacing, Frequent breaks, Peer assistance/cooperative learning, Assignment notebook, Preferential seating, Frequent positive reinforcement, Modified tests (format, oral, shortened), Extended or untimed tests and Additional material sent home. With these accommodations, Eric would have an Individualized Education Program (IEP) each year with goals and objectives discussed in a meeting with a teacher, school board representative and his parents.

When we saw Dr. Horton in November, we reported that Mrs. Taylor, Eric's teacher, was working with him on some tests and classroom assignments. She had learned that Eric would get confused when given too many choices and needed to have only three or four. She was allowing him to bring home science and health class work so we could help him study. "He needs to have material reinforced at home that he's had in class," I had written in my notes. Eric's ability to memorize, however, was still outstanding, and he already had learned all the multiplication and division facts.

Dr. Horton said although Eric was not exhibiting any OCD traits at the time, his ADHD symptoms might be affecting his grades, and she encouraged us to get specifics from his teacher.

We told Dr. Horton about our decision to leave the church where we were members and had been attending for years. For several Sundays, we had been visiting Lakeview United Methodist Church on Cross Lake in Shreveport, where we decided to join in January 1999, the same church where Rob's mom and I had attended the ADD seminar. Other than asking questions about why we were going to a different church, the boys seemed to be adjusting well to the new worship experience. We realized it might be a little difficult for them to leave a familiar church and familiar people, but they settled in quickly and made some new friends.

Not too long after we began attending Lakeview, Eric made the cover of the church's newsletter, *The Tie*. The Rev. Charles Humphreys, the pastor, was writing his column on an event that happened in church. It was a Sunday in which the congregation was invited to remember our baptism, and at the end of the service all people in attendance were invited to come forward to dip their hand in the water provided and touch their forehead.

"Most of us just used the tip of our fingers to touch the water," the Rev. Humphreys wrote, "but one little boy put both hands in the water and scooped it up in a generous fashion. I was thrilled with the way he entered into this 'remembrance' but also moved by the symbolic message of 'wash me and make me whiter than snow' it conveyed."

When Christmastime came, Eric printed his Santa list in neat letters and—true to Eric form—split his list into organized categories.

Eric Vardeman's List

Santa Claus List

Videos

Scooby Doo – A Nutcracker Scoob

Scooby Doo – The Haunted House Hang-Up

Computer Games

Jump Start 4th Grade

Jump Start 5th Grade

Colors

Markers (washable)

Books

Scooby Doo and the Snow Monster

Scooby Doo and the Sunken Ship

A Fifth Grade Spelling Book

Food

Candy canes

A gum machine

Paper

A 4-subject notebook (yellow)

Paper (loose-leaf)

Computer paper

Binders

A big purple binder

Chapter Eight

Gymnastics and a Best Friend

Eric had started taking gymnastics during the summer before third grade, and he was excelling in some of the stunts he was learning. He was good on the pullover, parallel bars and tumbling on the mats. He also worked and worked and worked until he could walk on his hands. He practiced all over our house, outside in the yard, at gymnastics and probably everywhere else he happened to be. His determination was amazing. He proved that hard work pays off because he learned to do it well and a few years later would participate in a talent show in middle school walking on his hands back and forth across the stage.

We reported to Dr. Horton on January 16, 1999, at our first appointment of the year that Eric had qualified for accommodations under Section 504, had barely passed his first speech and language screening and had scored poorly in reading comprehension. Comprehension deals with a lot of language, Dr. Horton pointed out, but not necessarily pragmatic (or practical) language, an area in which Eric had no problems. With Eric's ability to memorize, he easily understood subject-verb agreement, the parts of speech and the rules of language, such as "i" before "e" except after "c." However, with reading comprehension, Eric would have to think more deeply about what the words that form these sentences mean.

We also told Dr. Horton that we had been playing the card game "Go Fish" with Eric, and he was doing well because of his rote memory. He could remember who asked for what card, so that was an advantage for him. "He is taking his lunch to school and eating it," I had written in my notes. "He seems to have a great appetite right now."

For the first time in his life, Eric had a best friend, a cute red-haired, freckled-faced boy named Matthew Ogletree, and the two boys spent a lot of time together on the weekends and in their gymnastics classes. Matthew's limber frame was a lot like Eric's, and both boys excelled in the sport. Rob and I were thrilled that Eric had a good friend and that it was someone who shared his interest in gymnastics and the outdoors. We told Dr. Horton Eric was getting to sit beside Matthew in class and that seemed to be pleasing him. Also, Eric was happy because the class was studying multiplication. He had known all of the multiplication and division facts since the beginning of school and was ready for the rest of the class to catch up.

Memorizing the 50 states, the seven continents and the multiplication and division facts were easy for Eric, and he mastered these assignments with little effort in the third grade. With reading comprehension his greatest challenge, Eric was helped almost daily by Rob and me as we worked with him. The third grade reading book contained study book sheets with short stories and questions to answer, and we worked on these sheets at home.

Even though Eric had a somewhat rocky start at the beginning of the third grade, after he qualified for accommodations under Section 504, his grades improved and he made mostly "A's" and "B's" on his report card, with a few "C's" scattered around, mainly in reading. He received a 504 progress report from the Office of Special Programs on March 19, 1999, and the news was good. In language arts and social studies, Eric received scores of "2" (improving), and in science and health, he received "3's" (greatly improved). Under Recommendations and Comments, there were check marks beside Puts Forth Effort, Good Attitude, Well Behaved, Homework Completed and Follows Classroom/School Rules.

Eric had been Student of the Month in his class in October, received awards for Super Eagle, Principal's Honor Roll and physical education; a music trophy and completion certificates for Level 1 and Level 2 gymnastics; and several different ribbons for gymnastics. Also, this child—who a few years before had no desire to color inside the lines—was making "A's" in art, taking his time to create some beautiful work and showing some giftedness in the subject.

We saw Dr. Horton on March 4, a few days before Eric was scheduled to take the Iowa Test, and we reported that Eric would be able to take the test out of the classroom with an inclusion teacher and have additional time on each section of the test because of having qualified for accommodations under Section 504. We felt the additional time, in particular, would help Eric with reading comprehension. Dr. Horton reminded us that Eric sees things in a very concrete way and that his ability to understand abstract concepts and read between the lines would come with age as he matured. She probably was trying to prepare us in case his reading comprehension score was not where we expected it to be. When the test results were revealed, we were not surprised that Eric still needed a lot of work in reading comprehension.

At this visit, Dr. Horton wrote Eric a new prescription for Prozac. The prescription was for tablets. Eric was graduating from the liquid form of the drug to a "grown up" form. I remember thinking that one day I hope Eric will be able to graduate from having to take Prozac all together.

Eric and Kurt celebrated their ninth and fifth birthdays, respectively, together at a Chuck E. Cheese birthday party, complete with pizza, birthday cakes they decorated themselves and a special appearance by the Chuck E. Cheese mouse. Eric enjoyed the party and even danced with a girlfriend, holding her hands while they jumped around to the music. It was great seeing him interacting with his friends. We had a set of pullover bars erected in the backyard for Eric's birthday. He and his brother spent countless hours on the bars, doing flips and hanging upside down.

We took a spring break vacation to Santa Fe, New Mexico, the last week in March and spent a couple of days skiing on the slopes of the Sangre de Cristo Mountains. We put Eric in ski school and Kurt in Chipmunk Corner for kids. Eric was determined to learn to ski and worked so hard at it that he hyperventilated and had to have oxygen. By the second day, though, he was going up on the chair lift with us and skiing the green slopes. He was proud of his efforts and wanted me to watch him come down the hill with his dad nearby. "Look at me, Mother! Mother, look at me! Watch me," Eric said as he skied down the hill. I captured the Kodak moment with my camera.

Near the end of school, we were noticing that Eric was blinking his eyes excessively. He was doing this periodically for a few days at a time. He had gotten his braces on in May, and he couldn't keep his hands out of his mouth and off the new metal appliances. His current obsession was soft drinks and drink dispensing machines. We talked to Dr. Horton at Eric's appointment on May 27 about these issues as well as something else I was noticing: Eric didn't treasure anything. A track and field medal he received for running had been found on the floor in his room. The same thing happened with his toys. This disregard for possessions was more than "being a kid" and lacking maturity. Dr. Horton said it was an ADD trait, and we learned to accept it even though we tried to teach Eric to take care of his things. She wanted us to leave off his Ritalin after school was out for the summer.

The psychiatrist noted Eric was very talkative, was blinking his eyes and was "up on his toes" when he walked around in the clinic, the latter two of which were traits Eric had that waxed and waned throughout his young life.

Eric stayed busy during the summer of 1999 continuing his gymnastics classes and going swimming as often as possible. Our family and Rob's parents took our annual trip to the beach, this time to Destin, Florida, in June.

When we met with Dr. Horton in August shortly before school started, she put Eric back on Ritalin so he would be able to concentrate in class. I told her Eric had spent a lot of time during the summer making colored figures of various movie characters. He also was participating as an acolyte, a pastor's assistant, in church. In our church, there are several young people who go through a training program to serve as an acolyte, with the main responsibilities of lighting the candles on the altar at the beginning of the service and taking the light of Christ out at the end of the service. Eric willingly participated one Sunday but then given the choice of participating the next Sunday, he declined. We talked with him about his responsibility in serving God. After that, he was more willing to participate. Some of my favorite Sundays were when Eric, and later Kurt, served as acolytes. There aren't too many more special moments for a mom than to see her child in an acolyte robe walking down the center aisle of the church sanctuary looking like an angel.

Chapter Nine

The Reading Center, Mr. Maple and More Tests

We knew fourth grade would be a challenge because for the first time, Eric would be changing classes and having four teachers instead of one. During the first week of school in August, I scheduled a meeting with all of the teachers so I could talk about Eric. Even if I had not known what Eric's teachers looked like already, I would have been able to identify them because on the first day of school, Eric had drawn pictures of all four teachers and brought them home for us to see. He did a good job with the pictures, and although a bit crude, the drawings had a characteristic of each teacher featured. These drawings were also unique: I believe they were the only sketches of people Eric drew that year which didn't include tails.

Instead of meeting with the teachers individually, I was able to meet with them collectively, which made it easier to discuss Eric's particular needs and to let them know what we recently had done for him.

Earlier that month, Eric had undergone diagnostic reading and math testing at The Reading Center of Shreveport, and he had begun tutoring there twice a week. The test was given by Martha Maple, a reading specialist and fourth-grade reading teacher at Shreve Island Elementary School in Shreveport. Even though we had prepared Eric for the test, which took several hours and covered, among other areas, vocabulary, word recognition and comprehension, Mrs. Maple told us that Eric kept asking when his mother was going to pick him up. He was not a child who liked to sit still for very long, much less take a test that lasted several hours. The test results, dated August 7, 1999, showed Eric's strengths and weaknesses, as did other similar tests he had taken.

Mrs. Maple administered several tests on Eric: Slosson Intelligence Test-Revised (SIT-R), Peabody Picture Vocabulary Test-Third Edition (PPVT-III, Form A), Slosson Oral Reading Test-Revised (SORT-R), Classroom Reading Inventory (CRI, Form A), Developmental Test of Visual Motor Integration (VMI, 4th Revision), Gates-MacGinitie Reading Test (GMRT, Level 4, Form K) and Informal Dyslexia Screening Activities.

The six-page test results report began with a paragraph about Eric and included his age, parental information and where he attended school. The second paragraph explained how Eric came to be evaluated at The Reading Center and that he was under the care of Dr. Rita Horton, psychiatrist. Information taken from a conversation with me said Eric "reads well and can tell what the information is about but that he has problems sorting the information and pulling out certain parts. Mrs. Vardeman also stated that sometimes Eric doesn't give correct answers when he is asked specific questions. He appears to lack reasoning skills. Eric has been evaluated by the Office of Special Programs, Caddo Parish School Board, and qualifies under Section 504."

Eric's scores varied, just as they did on the dyslexia screening, generally ranking in the average to below-average range. Higher-than-average scores were in oral pronunciation of graded sight words and the SORT-R test, average scores were in the SIT-R and PPVT-III, and low scores were in the VMI and GMRT. In the Informal Dyslexia Screening Activities, Eric wrote his name, address and telephone number, the alphabet and copied a 29-word paragraph. He also correctly repeated the alphabet, months of the year and days of the week in sequence. In an informal auditory processing test, Eric repeated four of six sequences containing letters and numbers but had difficulty repeating the same letter/numeral sequences in reverse order. In a survey that estimates a student's attitude toward recreational and academic reading, Eric exhibited "a positive attitude toward both aspects of reading. However, he did indicate that he did not like to do workbook pages and worksheets." (Additional information and test scores are reported in the Appendix.)

In her report, Mrs. Maple included a "Behavioral Observations" paragraph in which she said Eric entered the testing situation willingly, was friendly and talkative, and "appeared to carefully, but readily, answer all questions throughout the evaluation." She said he was cooperative and seemed to put forth his best effort on each test section. He told Mrs. Maple he read some but was not an avid reader. He said he enjoyed reading about snakes and liked to play basketball and that the hardest thing about school was "when he got things wrong." Mrs. Maple wrote that before the end of the testing, Eric was "experiencing some anxiety about when he would be finished and if his mother had returned yet."

The report recommendation was that Eric receive one-on-one tutoring to improve his overall academic performance with the following objectives suggested for his specific tutorial plan:

To increase vocabulary understanding

To improve silent reading comprehension skills

To improve test-taking skills for standardized tests he will be taking as he

continues through school

To encourage and mentor Eric as he develops his pleasure reading skills to include a wide genre of literature

To develop Eric's process writing skills so that his reading and writing skills improve as he progresses through school

To improve math skills, especially in the area of word problems

To assist Eric at school, the following recommendations might be beneficial:

Make certain that Eric is looking at the teacher prior to directions being given. He needs to sit as close to the front as possible in order to be in close proximity to the teacher.

Utilize a homework assignment notebook to make sure all assignments are written down and completed. If necessary, the teacher should double-check to make sure Eric has his assignments written down correctly.

Make certain that Eric receives 504 modifications and accommodations in the classroom.

Encourage and monitor Eric as he develops his pleasure reading and writing. He should be reading for pleasure during the school day, as well as after school. He should have multiple opportunities to write during the school day.

To assist Eric at home, the following recommendations might be beneficial:

Provide support and assistance with homework and any other school-related work to ensure success in school. Eric should have an organized place to study, with the necessary supplies. Set up a regular study schedule and use the time to study even if homework is not assigned.

Encourage pleasure reading. Eric should be reading for a minimum of thirty minutes daily. Any book he reads should be read at his independent level, the level at which he misses no more than one or two words per page.

Encourage Eric to write for pleasure. He should have a Writer's Log in which he writes daily. He should be encouraged to write stories, poems and any other types of writing he finds interesting.

Maintain regular communication with Eric's teachers in order to monitor his progress closely. A daily checklist might prove beneficial in order to monitor his progress in all subjects on a daily basis.

The report also recommended that we consider evaluation for supportive services through the special education inclusion program. If he were an inclusion student, Eric would qualify for supportive services within the classroom and during testing. "Achievement testing will be a vital part of Eric's academic progress from now on and he deserves the opportunity to receive as much instructional support as possible," the report noted.

The report concluded with the following paragraph:

Eric is a delightful young man who has strong academic potential. He should be encouraged in every way to be a successful student. He should begin to take responsibility for his pleasure reading and writing. Research has shown that daily reading and writing are the most effective ways to improve student achievement in these areas.

We began Eric's tutoring immediately two days a week at the Reading Center. Eric's tutor was Mrs. Maple's husband, Richard, a career educator and former principal at an Arkansas school. Mr. Maple became one of Eric's best pals. He had a gentle way with Eric and knew how to get the best work out of him. Mr. Maple instilled in our son a love for reading while helping Eric understand what he was reading. The tutor learned about Asperger's Syndrome and how best he could help Eric with his special needs. He also found Eric did his best when he was not confined to a seat at a desk. Mr. Maple let him roam around the room and answer questions orally. When Mr. Maple had to travel out of town and had a substitute take his place at tutoring one week, he told the sub, "Whatever you do, don't make him sit in a chair." The educator understood Eric and his needs, and Eric appreciated him for it.

When I met with Eric's teachers, I told them about the diagnostic testing, tutoring at the Reading Center and how having Asperger's Syndrome affected Eric and what they might expect in the classroom. I told them even though Eric had a vivid imagination, he would give a one- or two-word answer to critical thinking questions. I asked them to keep me informed of any problems, behavioral changes or tics they noticed so we could consider a change in his medication. I also emphasized Eric needed to know in advance of any changes in the daily school schedule. "He is very routine-oriented," I wrote in my notes. "He will ask questions to try to understand why things are different. For example, an assembly." I explained when I would ask Eric what happened at school that day, he would tell me everything that was different from the normal routine but nothing such as "I made an "A" on my test or I won the race in the 100-yard dash." The teachers were all very understanding and expressed willingness to help Eric as much as they could. They also mentioned we might pursue getting an aid to work with Eric in the classroom. This was a great suggestion because he already was having some problems staying organized with having to change classes. The teachers also gave me an extra set of books to keep at home in case Eric forgot to bring home the ones he needed for homework assignments.

For an aide to be assigned to Eric, I had to request an emergency evaluation through a letter to Susan Taylor, the Caddo Parish special education director. In the letter, I explained about Eric's diagnosis of Asperger's Syndrome, told why we were seeking the emergency evaluation and gave some background information on Eric. The special education office also received a copy of the test results from The Reading Center which were forwarded to the School Building Level Committee (SBLC) and to the Pupil Appraisal representative at the school.

The next step was to have the SBLC conduct and document screening activities. More forms were filled out including a parental permission form for initial evaluation. This form gave permission for the following evaluations for Eric:

• Vision and/or Hearing Screening, if not previously conducted.

• Review and analysis of screening information including school attendance, educational, social and medical history.

• Interviews with the student, the family and the teacher(s) if in school.

• Observation of the student during daily activities, such as in the classroom, on the playground, at lunch, at home, etc.

• Appropriate tests which are designed to measure different types of abilities and may include individually administered tests of general knowledge and/or academic ability.

• Other assessments, if found to be needed during the course of the evaluation.

Cynthia Williams, Blanchard Elementary's coordinator, completed another form for the SBLC that included screening information and academic/educational history, with academic strengths listed as *willing to work, spelling, capitalization, punctuation, "concrete" information, math-basic skills, social skills.* Under the social skills section of the form, Eric's classroom behavior was described as *shy, quiet; wants to please, looks like he understands and usually doesn't ask questions.* Concerns were listed as note-taking and weakness in comprehension of materials and processing.

We met with Dr. Horton for an appointment on October 9 and reported that Eric was undergoing an evaluation to see if he could qualify for an aide. We also told her he was being tutored at The Reading Center and progress already was being made. The focus, we told her, is on silent reading comprehension and to get him ready for the spring Louisiana Educational Assessment Program (LEAP) test for fourth-graders. This test was important: Eric would have to score Approaching Basic or above in both the English Language Arts and Mathematics tests to advance to fifth grade.

We told her Eric was eating and sleeping well, his teachers reported good attention in class, and we were working on reading comprehension at home 30 minutes a day. Dr. Horton asked about any tics he was having, and I said he had a little hum tic now and then.

Following the Dr. Horton appointment, I wrote a letter to his four teachers on October 11.

We visited Eric's doctor over the weekend and she wanted me to check with all of you on whether his attention is good throughout the day. I always share samples of Eric's class work with her. I showed her a copy of a reading assignment where he made an "A+" on one side and an "F" on the other, and she thought perhaps his attention waned from the time he started the first side to the time he ended the second side. He is a good deal bigger than he was in the third grade, and he still is taking the same dosage of Ritalin. Dr. Horton did not change his medicine dosage yet but wanted me to check with all of you on his attention. Sometimes he can appear to have good attention but doesn't really have it. Please let me know so that we can increase his medication if necessary. Not enough Ritalin can cause a decrease in attention but too much can cause hyperactivity. Sometimes it's hard to get the balance right. Thank you all for your continuing help. I really appreciate it.

The paperwork has been signed and the process is underway for testing by the Office of Special Programs (in the effort to provide an aide to work with Eric). They are going to try to do the testing during enrichment times so he won't have to miss class. I don't know how long the testing process will take.

Eric's first mid-period progress report in the fourth grade showed him with all "A's" and "B's" except for a "C" in health and a "B-" in reading. We were happy with the reading grade and knew it indicated a lot of improvement for him. Tutoring was paying off in a big way. His 504 progress report showed he was improving in all subjects.

On October 19, I received a note from Michele Burgess, Eric's math teacher. The note read:

Mrs. Vardeman,

Eric seems to be doing fine in my room with his attention. I don't see where increasing his medication would help him in any way. He's doing great!

Michele Burgess

At our December appointment with Dr. Horton, I reported Eric had been more hyperactive at home, even though his teachers were not noticing a problem in the classroom. "He seems to be about ready to burst," I wrote in my notes. "It's harder for him to sit still and concentrate when we study, and even his playtime is more active and reckless than it was."

I told Dr. Horton that Janet Brown from the Office of Special Programs had completed testing and observing Eric in the classroom and a report would be forthcoming. Ms. Brown had discussed with me some examples of the test questions and Eric's answers. These answers were interesting and showed how Eric related each situation to himself. He was given a visual (picture), and Ms. Brown asked him questions about it. One was a picture of a child and a doctor, and he was told the pre-school child is visiting the doctor so he can get a checkup to enter school. When asked about it, Eric said the dentist is changing the wires on his teeth. Having recently had braces put on his teeth, Eric related the child in the picture to himself and his world. When asked what "check up" means, Eric said the child is getting signed up for school. The next picture was unrelated to the first one, but when asked about it, Eric was still stuck on the first picture and his answer reflected that. Another sample question from the same test was about recycling, and Eric said recycling was taking cans to get money for them. He did not understand the concept of recycling as helping the environment. He had been with his dad to a recycling center and received money in exchange for the aluminum, so he again related the situation to his life.

Ms. Brown told me that we needed to find ways to help Eric relate abstract things to literal things because he understands literal concepts. In problem solving, if it is abstract, make it concrete, she explained. Role-playing was encouraged as was setting up rules for Eric to follow in social situations. I had talked to Ms. Brown about Eric's hyperactivity, and she told me we should not stop Eric from doing certain things such as bumping his chair on the floor because it is his way of calming himself down.

I relayed to Dr. Horton that Eric tended to "get stuck" more than he had been. A new pastime for Eric was cutting out figures and having them "fight" with each other. He would cut out hundreds of the creatures, some he colored and some he left uncolored, and he would have them fight each other usually until one of them was torn to shreds. "It is hard to get him to stop," I told Dr. Horton. The psychiatrist increased Eric's Prozac dosage slightly in hopes that it would help Eric's tendency of "getting stuck" to subside. She also slightly increased his Ritalin.

Dr. Horton noticed that Eric appeared anxious and had decreased eye contact and interaction.

A behavior evaluation sheet was given to me by Dr. Horton to give to Eric's teachers. The Vanderbilt Teacher Behavior Evaluation Scale gave the teacher an opportunity to score the student in 35 areas including the following: Fails to give attention to details or makes careless mistakes in schoolwork, has difficulty sustaining attention in tasks or activities, has difficulty organizing tasks or activities and is easily distracted by extraneous stimuli. The scale also included questions as to bullying, guilt feelings and depression. We were thankful none of Eric's teachers indicated he had any problems in these areas.

Kay Cochran, Eric's physical education teacher, wrote the following comments:

Eric's behavior and peer relationships have changed over the past three months...seems unaware of class environment and this leads to poor peer relationships. All of Eric's teachers should be informed of his strengths and weaknesses and along with Eric's parents set up his goals and objectives for next school year.

I adore Eric. Obviously I am not aware of his classroom behaviors and achievement. I am concerned about his ability to relate to his peers. His physical abilities appear to be normal but it would be wise to evaluate his physical skills. (We can do this at school). Eric is lucky to have parents like you and your husband. Stay on top of Eric's strengths and weaknesses. Let me know if I can do anything else.

Mrs. Cochran had worked with Eric on walking properly when he was younger and had a tendency to walk on his toes. She continued to keep me up-to-date on his progress as he grew older.

I wrote another letter to Eric's teachers on December 7, including some of the same concerns I had recently mentioned to Dr. Horton:

Eric's appointment with Dr. Rita Horton, his psychiatrist, is scheduled for Saturday, Dec. 11, and I wanted to know if there are any concerns you have regarding his behavior, progress in class, etc., that we need to share with her. His progress in class is fairly easy for us to monitor because of the weekly progress reports. What I am mainly concerned with is whether he seems more hyperactive (shifting in his seat, bumping his chair on the floor, etc.) than he did at the first of school. I've noticed a change at home. He seems to be about ready to burst. It's harder for him to sit still and concentrate when we study, and even his playtime is more active and reckless than it was. Janet Brown from the Office of Special Programs has told me that we should not stop him from doing certain things such as bumping his chair on the floor because it is his way of calming himself down. This is, however, something I need to share with Dr. Horton. If there is anything at all that concerns you about Eric, it will also concern me, so please let me know if there are any problems.

Thank you all for everything you are doing for Eric—the classroom accommodations and other help you are giving him. The Office of Special Programs testing and observing is complete, and we should be getting a written evaluation/report within the next couple of weeks. I will share that report with all of you if you don't get one from their office.

Later in December, the long-awaited report from the Office of Special Programs was ready. After I was given a copy of the confidential document, I realized why it took so long to complete. It was a 14-page document, mostly single-spaced and very thorough.

The first page of the report contained general information about Eric, such as his date of birth, school, grade, parents' names and address. It listed the primary exceptionality as "autism—Asperger's Syndrome" with secondary exceptionalities of "speech impairments: language." Other impairments/conditions listed weak abstract reasoning and comprehension, mild-moderate language delay and weak social skills. The next page had the reason for referral:

Eric is a 9-year-old student in the 4th grade at Blanchard Elementary School. He was referred because of concerns regarding weak academic progress. In addition, social difficulties were identified. Eric reportedly demonstrated an atypical learning style that required much one-to-one help at school and home.

The report said the school psychologist had reviewed the SBLC screening data, which indicated Eric had demonstrated weak academic performance and atypical social skills over an extended period of time. Eric's vision and hearing were normal, and his general health was good, according to the report. School-based screening results showed adequate communication and motor skills. Eric exhibited "very mild symptoms of sensory processing difficulties such as putting his hands over his ears when there is too much noise, grimaces as task difficulty increases, difficulty transitioning and distractibility," the report said, but these were being appropriately managed and there was no need for further intervention.

The 504 accommodations that began in February 1999 were listed:

Eric will be given repeated directions on classroom assignments and tests.

Eric may use listening center for reinforcement of reading text stories.

Eric will be given a few items at a time on classwork and tests.

Eric will be given extended time in content area for classwork and tests.

Eric will be given an example (do one with him) on classwork and tests.

Eric will have tests read aloud as needed.

The school psychologist had reviewed his grades as well as the results of his Iowa Test from third grade and had performed a teacher interview in which Eric was described as a "generally cooperative and polite student." He was said to follow classroom rules, to conform to teacher's behavioral expectations, and to have adequate motivation and a sincere desire to do well at school. Social concerns were his difficulty relating to other students in social settings and lack of knowledge in developing and maintaining typical friendships. Academic weaknesses were listed in reading comprehension, oral expression, comprehension, and extracting details and organizing his thoughts and materials. Weak peer relations was a behavioral concern.

The report included a summary of a parent interview, extracted from information and my answers to questions asked by a social worker, which included the following: Eric's diagnosis of Asperger's, the medication he was taking for OCD and ADHD, problems in organizational skills, strengths including his rote memory skills, social activities, birth history, health care, family relations, tutoring at the Reading Center and my desire to have an aide assist Eric with his organizational skills.

The school psychologist reviewed Eric's 504 evaluation and IEP, revealing the following educational profile:

Poor ability to process lecture material; average cognitive ability; personal characteristics of shyness, unassertive, easily distracted; weak spelling, neatness in work and weak written expression. Overall, Eric seems to know material but performs poorly on tests. He appears disorganized in tasks and thinking. He has difficulty expressing himself orally and in "retrieving" words. He appears to read but not comprehend. Eric qualified for

82

504 accommodations and his plan included the six objectives noted earlier in this report. Implementation of his plan began in 2/99, and his teachers continue to consistently provide accommodations as needed. Eric is successful in school under this plan.

An additional area addressed by his teachers relates to Eric's personal tendencies to have difficulty with transitions or less structured settings. He had been described as rushing through a task, thus missing details of instructions; he needs assurance that unfinished work can be dealt with at a later time; he might not ask for help but obviously misses the mark in understanding instructions. Eric's teachers provide appropriate interventions to deal with these issues, resulting in his good grades.

The next part of the report dealt with Eric's academic performance. The tests used were the Woodcock-Johnson-Revised, Tests of Achievement, Selected Subtests (W-J-R), Curriculum-Based Assessment and Informal Assessment. Eric was tested in the areas of reading, math and written expression/language. Through the teacher interview, it was noted that Eric had the most difficulty with his skills in reading comprehension, understanding of overall directions and organizational skills. Additional information was gathered through a curriculum-based assessment and review of classroom curriculum expectations, and that information indicated Eric was making adequate progress at the instructional level expected. (Complete test results follow in the Appendix.)

One section of the report dealt with characteristics and behaviors exhibited by Eric that could be classified as "autistic." The first paragraph of this section follows:

Eric is reported to have been exhibiting autistic-like characteristics since at least his preschool years. He was diagnosed with obsessive-compulsive disorder and his mother noted some stereotypic twirling of thread, looking at ceiling fans and toe-walking. A review of Eric's school records indicate that his school adjustment problem, autistic-like characteristics and comprehension difficulties are long-term. His 504 evaluation documents adequate cognitive ability.

83

The report said Eric was diagnosed with Asperger's Syndrome by a licensed physician, that he was receiving routine pediatric care, his general health was good, hearing was adequate and hearing deficits were never suspected.

The following significant identifying characteristics suggesting the probability of an autism (Asperger's) classification were noted through teacher interviews:

- *Eric cannot take a large section of material and group it into smaller units;*

- *He is more likely to complete written language work accurately than to tell you about it;*

- *He cannot logically or in an organized way tell you about a concept;*

- *He goes through written work compulsively in his effort to finish it – it's often inaccurate;*

- *Disorganized, clueless about how to organize his materials, desks, backpack;*

- *Eric can read but does not understand the concepts;*

- *He fixates on nonclass activity;*

- *He is anxious when he has to discontinue unfinished work temporarily;*

- *Eric is not a social/cooperative learner; unassertive; does not seem to know social rules to be able to establish and maintain friends;*

- *Eric is unable to actively participate in group activities or hands-on projects, due to social context;*

- *He does not understand the lessons on an abstract level; he is unable to process and apply information.*

Upon classroom observation, Eric was on task 80% of the time, according to the report. As tasks became more difficult, slight rocking in his chair and facial grimaces were noted. During an interview, Eric seemed unable to answer questions "richly" but he was willing to participate with the examiner, the report noted. He told the examiner, he sometimes "needs help in reading and social studies."

The report said a determination of Eric's learning styles showed he learns best with rules, structures, visual cues, concrete examples, breaking down large units into smaller bits and minimizing abstract concepts. Also, organization must be provided for him.

Another part of the report was a behavior assessment, conducted to identify specific characteristics that relate to Eric's Asperger's Syndrome. The report noted the following significant behaviors:

• *Difficulty developing interpersonal relationships, lack of awareness of another's feelings;*

• *Never plays with toys appropriately, never asks for toys, has no prized possessions;*

• *Rigidly follows rules; poor in transitions;*

• *Has no awareness of social trends;*

• *Does not comprehend jokes, sarcasm, irritation;*

• *Repetitive rocking, hands in mouth, grimaces.*

Considering all of the data, "It was the examiner's conclusion that Eric exhibits a mild degree of autistic behavior or characteristics. Eric's profile seems most appropriately identified by the term Asperger's Syndrome, as determined by the Dr. Rita Horton."

Strengths and support needs were listed in the report as follows:

Strengths:

> *Good conduct at school*

> *Follows rules well*

> *Concerned/supportive parents*

> *Grade appropriate academic skills*

> *Excellent rote memory skills*

> *School motivation*

Support Needs:

> *Weak reasoning and problem-solving skills*

> *Difficulty separating/reducing broad blocks of material into smaller conceptual units*

> *Weak abstract thinking skills*

> *Weak social skills*

> *Mild-moderate language delay (pragmatic skills and comprehension)*

The Eligibility/Integrated Summary portion of the report listed information about Eric, the reason for evaluation referral and academic assessment. "It is important to note that Eric's current 504 accommodation plan plays an integral part in his educational success and should be continued as needed in each of his regular classrooms," the report said.

With Eric's exhibition of a mild degree of autistic behavior, disturbances were noted in the areas of communication, relating to people, events and/or objects and repetitive patterns of behavior.

Under Communication, the report listed the following:

Disturbances in developing interpersonal relationships

Marked impairment in the use and understanding of nonverbal and symbolic communication.

The second area, Relating to people, events and/or objects, listed five disturbances:

Difficulty in developing interpersonal relationships

Impairments in awareness of the existence of others and their feelings

Absent capacity to use objects (e.g., toys) functionally and to assign them symbolic or thematic meaning

Difficulty generalizing and/or discerning inappropriate versus appropriate

behavior across settings and situations

Difficulty comprehending other's social/communication intentions (e.g., doesn't understand jokes, sarcasm, etc.).

The third area, Repetitive patterns of behaviors, listed two problems:

Marked distress over change or transitions

Repetitive motor movements (rocking, popping his chair, grimaces).

The report noted the disturbances are not due to mental disability, specific sensory deficits, aphasia (a disorder caused by damage to parts of the brain that are responsible for language), or physical or psychological trauma.

After reviewing all data, the report said, "It is the consensus of the team that Eric meets the criteria for the exceptionality of Autism with a secondary exceptionality of Speech Impairments: Language."

With the exception of several signature pages, the last page of the report was titled "Needs/Recommendations" and is as follows:

1. *a. Improve reasoning and problem-solving skills in order to improve overall classroom functioning.*

   b. Educational/Parental

   c. Provide visual cues, role playing, explanations of details. Use   concrete examples and as much visual support as possible.

2. *a. To improve language skills.*

   b. Educational/Speech and Language Services

   c. Interventions should include:

      1. Activities to improve problem-solving abilities by expressing logical and reasonable answers to questions.

      2. Activities to aid in comprehension of implied meanings.

      3. Activities to increase higher level vocabulary and comprehension skills.

      4. Visual support (written rules) and role-playing, whenever possible,

   should aid in comprehension of social situations.

      5. Activities to increase pragmatic language skills. (Topic maintenance, turn-taking, greetings, etc.)

3. *a. Improve skills in social interactions.*

   b. Educational/Parental

c. Role play situations; practice social rules.

We were very grateful for the report and happy that Eric would have more assistance. While the school, teachers and support personnel had some requirements to fulfill, we had some challenging work ahead of us as well. The challenge was not a concern for Rob or me, though, because we would do whatever it took to help our son.

Chapter Ten

Scooby Doo, Tabasco Sauce and Papa Bear

One thing I found helpful for Eric was to make up practice tests for vocabulary and reading that would also serve as study guides for classroom tests. This was something I used in high school and college that helped me greatly. It was a lot of work, but I didn't mind. If it helped Eric, I certainly was willing to take the time. I enjoyed being able to make up sentences for Eric's vocabulary words and use familiar names, like his, Kurt's and our dog, Lucy's. Eric was not always happy to take these practice tests, but he enjoyed writing his score on the top of the page, particularly if he made a 100%.

Eric was drawing constantly during this time, and a favorite subject of his was Scooby Doo, the talking cartoon dog, and his friends, who were known for solving mysteries. He loved to collect Scooby Doo video tapes and sketch Scooby and his friends, Freddie, Daphne, Velma and Shaggy. With some of these drawings, Eric would include the words from the VHS box covers, such as "Cartoon Network, Classic Scooby Doo." Occasionally, we found Eric replaced the original box with his own version, making a box out of paper in the exact dimensions of the original. Eric also wrote his own Scooby Doo mystery stories, complete with Scooby's language impairment of beginning each main word with an "r" sound, such as, "I ron't rike to rolve rysteries (I don't like to solve mysteries)."

Although Eric gave one- or two-word answers to critical thinking questions, he showed a lot of imagination with his writing. Usually involving an animal, Eric's stories were interesting. He made an "A" on this one, written in November 1999, and it involved a bull:

Robin and the Bull

by Eric Vardeman

Robin was a little boy who loved to fight bulls. One day he went to the fair. Robin saw a crode (crowd) of people waiting to fight bulls. Robin paid the man his ticket and went in. The man said, "in a minute I will shoot the gun." Robin waited a few minutes. Soon the man shot the gun. The gate opened and the bulls stepped out. All the people were scared except Robin. Everyone ran from the bulls. Robin ran for a little while and then stopped. Robin shouted, "I'm not afraid of you," he said. The bull was mad. He leaped over Robin. Robin said that was a close one. The bull leaped over Robin again. When the bull landed on the ground, Robin ran up and grabbed the bull's leg. He swung the bull very fast and let him go. He flew threw (through) the sky and got his horn stuck in a tree. Everybody cheered for Robin. He made a great big smile.

As Eric continued in fourth grade, we began to notice a distinction between the tests teachers administered to Eric orally through his 504 accommodation plan as opposed to the ones he took that were not read aloud to him. He scored much higher on the oral tests. Apparently the oral tests were easier for his brain to process.

In January 2000 at mid-term, after meeting with the principal, we decided to transfer Eric into a new class—one where he would have only one teacher and not change classes. We thought this change would help Eric because he would not have to work so hard to stay organized. Organization was extremely important because if a student was changing classes, he had to remember which books to get out of his locker for which classes. His reading teacher taught only reading, but the other teachers taught more than one subject.

What we didn't realize was changing classes was good for Eric because it helped him be less restless. Also, when we moved him to the new class, it disrupted his routine, and he had a difficult time adjusting. The teacher, Melanie Johnston, had a teaching style that was not as structured as Eric was accustomed, and that was difficult for him. For instance, reading was scheduled from

8:30 a.m. to 10 a.m. Mondays and Fridays and from 9 a.m. to 10:30 a.m. on Tuesdays, Wednesdays and Thursdays. On Fridays, language/spelling class was interrupted by a 30-minute library time.

There were only 15 students in the new class, so that was a plus for Eric. Mrs. Johnston was young and energetic, and Eric liked her. He did very well at first in her class, and he was making good grades. On a mid-period progress report In February, Eric grades were all "A's" and "B's," and he had check marks beside "Is doing excellent work," "Is completing all assignments" and "Has good work habits and citizenship." Under teacher comments, Mrs. Johnston had written, "He's truly a joy to teach! He's the sweetest child I've ever had the pleasure to know!" I added under parent comments: "I'm glad to hear that Eric is doing so well. He's fortunate to have been able to get in your class. Thank you for everything."

With Eric's having accommodations in the classroom, he received a special education progress report from Caddo Parish Schools showing goals and objectives completed by his inclusion teacher, Kim Thomas. The report showed Eric was improving in all areas except one—follow oral/written directions—which showed "needs improving." Beside that score, Mrs. Thomas had written:

Directions are repeated and written on the board, but individual attention is required. Therefore, Eric needs improvement due to the fact of no past history to compare.

On January 24, Rob and I met with teachers, the speech therapist, school coordinator and school board representative for Eric's IEP. Areas covered were his strengths, support needs, parental concerns, evaluation results, progress in general curriculum, statewide assessment results, consideration of special factors including transition program needs, curriculum adaptations/modifications and specialized equipment. The IEP report listed them as follows:

Strengths: On intelligence screenings, Eric's mental age equivalent was 9.5 which measured at his chronological age. He has a strength in comprehension of everyday events. He utilizes good decoding strategies to pronounce words and has great rote memory skills.

Support needs: Eric has difficulty with questions requiring short-term auditory memory and similarities/differences. Difficulties were also recognized in developing interpersonal relationships and comprehending others' feelings, jokes or sarcasms. Change brings distress.

Parental concerns: Eric attends tutoring twice a week and is helped much at home. Parents would like to see more services and support at school with more individualized attention.

Evaluation results: Eric has been successful with 504 accommodations since 2/99; however, interventions began much earlier. Problems remained with transitions, his rushing through tasks, need for reassurance that unfinished work can be done later and his not asking for help.

Progress in general curriculum: All grades for the 1ˢᵗ nine-week period of 4ᵗʰ grade were A's and B's with a GPA of 3.7. He has been successful in a departmentalized setting with 504 modifications and organizational assistance from teachers and inclusion aide. For second semester, Eric has been moved to a self-contained classroom, 4ᵗʰ grade regular ed with 15 students.

Statewide assessment results: IOWA testing shows skills lie between average and high. Lowest scores are in science and math concepts/estimate; Highest, capitalization. Subtests requiring improvement include history, library catalog system and strategies in data interpretation.

Consideration of special factors: Due to Asperger's Syndrome, Eric often remains confused in class or misinterprets instructions. Things that come naturally to other students do not come naturally to him. Difficulties exist in development of interpersonal relationships and generalizing inappropriate/non-appropriate behaviors.

Curricular adaptations/modifications: Eric learns best with rules, structures, visual cues, concrete examples, breaking down large units into smaller bits and minimizing abstract concepts. Organizational tasks require assistance. He has difficulty expressing himself and in "retrieving" words.

Specialized equipment: No specialized equipment is required, but specialized assistance is. Eric requires preferential seating in close proximity of his teacher. He has marked distress over change or transitions, making assistance in organizational tasks a must.

The IEP report included accommodations for the upcoming spring standardized LEAP test. Four accommodations were listed for Eric: Tests read aloud except reading comprehension, extended time, individual/small group and repeated directions.

Modifications and accommodations needed for regular classes in five areas were listed: environment, teaching strategies, materials, time demands and behavior concerns.

Under environment, the following modifications were named: assign preferential seating, alter physical room environment, use learning centers, use notebook for assignments/materials/homework, provide individualized/small group instruction, assign peer tutors/work buddies/note takers, reduce/minimize distractions, consider alternative grouping, stand near the student when giving directions or correcting, and provide adaptive equipment.

Modifications in the other areas named were to teach to the student's learning style (visual), modify/repeat/model directions, increase the amount of time to complete assignments and tests, provide cues and prepare for transitions in daily activities, and provide instruction in social skills.

Four short-term objectives with a goal of 80% accuracy were listed as follows:

Given visual or auditory stimuli, Eric will give appropriate answers to problem-solving questions about everyday situations.

Given auditory/visual stimuli, Eric will verbally express comprehension of specific vocabulary words.

Given visual and auditory stimuli, Eric will use appropriate conversational structuring, turn taking, repair and topic management in conversational tasks appropriate to age level.

Given visual or auditory stimuli, Eric will complete a story web or similar strategy to identify key points in a specific text.

Eric's speech therapist, Mary Beth Tucker, gave me a copy of something she was using when working with Eric, called The Four Maxims of Conversational Interaction (Twachtman, 1996, based upon the work of Grice, 1975). She called them our "rules" for conversation and suggested we use them at home when working with Eric.

Maxim One is Quantity, *the rule to be informative without being verbose. Speaking "non-stop" without regard to "social distress" signals is an example of difficulty with quantity.* "Keep it simple," Mrs. Tucker wrote beside Maxim One.

The second maxim is Quality. *The rule to be truthful. Confabulation (i.e., filling in knowledge gaps with false information that the speaker believes to be true) is an example of difficulty with quality.* "Keep it truthful," she wrote beside that maxim.

Maxim Three is Relevance. *The rule to contribute only information that is pertinent to the topic and situation. Tangential comments constitute difficulty with the rule of relevance.* "Stay with the subject," she wrote beside Maxim Three.

Maxim Four is Clarity. *The rule that the information conveyed is clear and understandable to the listener. Initiating a conversation in the middle of a thought, without providing background information, is an example of a problem with the rule of clarity.* "Explain carefully," Mrs. Tucker wrote.

We were grateful for Mrs. Tucker as well as Eric's teachers and others who shared helpful aids with us. Eric would not have progressed nearly as quickly without these helps and suggestions.

With his writing, Eric continued to show creativity. A conversation with him usually didn't bring out this trait, but when he had the opportunity to write, he could bring his world to life. A paragraph about being invisible got him a 98% and a "very good" comment from Mrs. Johnston written at the top:

I would like to be invisible. Being invisible is cool, because I could sneak in the kitchen at night and get some food. I would be very quiet so that I wouldn't wake Mom and Dad. After I got the food, I would take it to my room and eat it. I'd have to be invisible to sneak food because if I was not, somebody might catch me.

I'm sure when Eric was writing his paragraph, he was remembering my rule of no food anywhere in the house except in the kitchen and dining room. To Eric, rules were something people were supposed to follow, and he was not a person to deviate from the rules. He might not agree with them, but he certainly would follow them. He never took a glass of milk or a potato chip bag to his room.

To his brother, Kurt, however, rules very often meant something that you might follow or you might not depending on how you felt at the time. On more than one occasion, Kurt got into trouble because I would find plastic baggies with cookies or chips in them in his room. I even found in his toy box a plastic drink box with a straw that had once held milk—or at least I think it was milk. The drink box was the source of a very bad smell coming from his room, and although I was glad to have found the problem, it almost made me sick. What was a little funny about the story, though, is that Kurt did not know how long it had been there and didn't even remember taking the drink box into his room. Knowing him, he probably tried to blame it on one of his friends. But he knew better than to try to pin it on his brother because Eric would never have done something like that. One of our favorite quotes of Eric's is about the subject of "messing up." He would say, "He shouldn't have done that." Eric found out early in his life that people don't always do what they should. He used that quote quite often. Our family picked up on it, and we repeat it when someone does something wrong, whether intentionally or accidentally.

Rob and I continued to read articles and books on developmental disorders, ADD and ADHD. During the first part of 2000, I attended a seminar with Dr. Mark Cogburn, a family therapist with the Behavioral Medicine and Learning Clinic in Shreveport. The title was "ADD/ADHD: Parenting Tops for ages 3-10." Dr. Cogburn discussed parenting techniques that are helpful for effective discipline and encouraging good behavior and self-control.

Some of the key points I learned from Dr. Cogburn:

A philosophy of providing a safe, structured environment offers the opportunity to make choices that result in learning.

ADHD kids need structure but they don't like it; allow them to make choices.

In behavior management, the two needs are the right motivation and a plan.

Freedom and responsibility go together.

Punishment should be severe, intense, short in duration and infrequently used.

Rewards keep the good behavior going and work better than punishment.

Grounding doesn't work as well as restriction: take away the television, movies or CD players or have the child wash your car. Make the child realize he's being punished.

Don't argue and explain; use "because I said so."

Make the plan work through setting limits, being consistent, following through, voice control and monitoring closely.

Don't tell the child, "You don't want to know what's going to happen." Make it specific.

The home should be a parent-centered home and not a child-centered home.

Give them something with the threat of taking it away, such as a limited number of coins. Take one away if the child doesn't do his homework.

A child has the right to shelter, clothing, food and not to be abused. He does not have the right to his own room. If he's destructive, take his room away from him and let him sleep on the floor.

The information was valuable, and I felt my evening at the seminar was well spent. We began using Dr. Cogburn's tips at home and continued to use them in the years to come. Not only was the information good for parents with an ADD/ADHD child, but also it was good advice for all parents and caregivers of children.

* * * * *

For his 10th birthday, Eric got a new silver and red Huffy bicycle, and we celebrated both boys' birthdays with parties at home with family and at the skating rink with friends.

Even as a toddler, Eric never played with toys the way they were designed.

Tiny hands turn light switches on and off. Over and over.

Santa himself can't keep Eric interested.

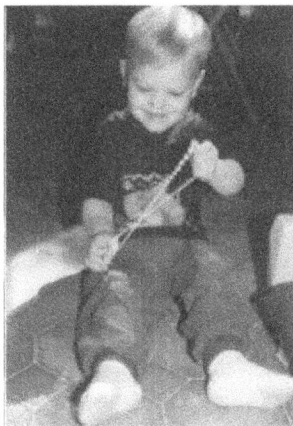

Eric plays with "beebs."

The alphabet was something Eric learned by age two.

Eric loved books at an early age.

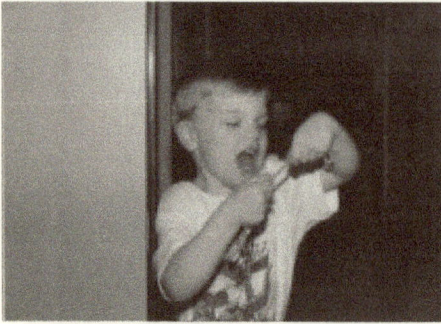

At age three, Eric twirls a string of Mardi Gras beads and sings a list of songs.

At three-year-old preschool, Eric keeps his distance from his classmates.

Eric's cute crooked grin at age four shows his cross-bite.

One of Eric's favorite Halloween costumes—a Dalmation.

Eric with teacher Shelley Lowery in first grade on his birthday.

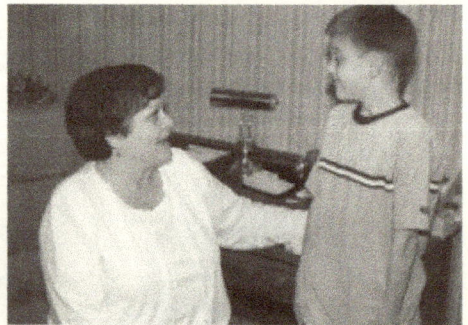

Child and Adolescent Psychiatrist Dr. Rita Horton with Eric (age nine) in 1999.

Eric and Richard Maple, his tutor and pal at The Reading Center of Shreveport.

Eric with instructor Jason at gymnastics

Shelly Walters, Eric's reading teacher at Blanchard Elementary School, and Eric on his 11th birthday in 2001.

Eric and his friend, Matthew Ogletree, eating pizza to celebrate Eric's 11th birthday.

Eric and Grandmother Jones on his 12th birthday.

On Confirmation Sunday in 2001, Eric's classmates are a little too close for comfort. Eric is second from right.

Eric lights a candle as part of his induction into the National Junior Honor Society at Calvary Baptist Academy.

Eric and his buddy Stinson Bundrick with their senior rings in May 2007.

Eric and Kurt on Eric's high school graduation day in May 2008. Eric wears National Honor Society and Beta Club collars.

We also took a spring break vacation to South Louisiana and enjoyed a swamp tour on an air boat and a tour of the Tabasco factory at Avery Island. A variety of wildlife was spotted on the swamp tour including several varieties of birds, an owl that stayed perched on a high tree branch, and, of course, lots of alligators. The Tabasco factory tour was interesting and was exciting for Eric, who, when given a tiny sample bottle of Tabasco, climbed a tree and drank the contents of the bottle. Like one of the birds we had seen on the swamp tour, Eric "flew" out of the tree, ran to me red-faced and told me his mouth was burning. Seeing the empty bottle in his hands, I knew what he had done and was shocked. I thought he knew Tabasco sauce was hot, but I guess he thought the contents of such a tiny bottle couldn't be that hot. We headed for the water fountain and after a few minutes, the redness in his face was gone and he calmed down.

* * * * *

Part of the progress Eric made at the first of the year was stalled by the fourth nine weeks of school, when Eric started becoming lazy in class. His sloppy handwriting was proving it.

Eric brought home a sheet of notebook paper containing his large, sloppy printing. I sent it back to school with him the next day with a note to his teacher:

Mrs. Johnston,

I don't know how you read this terrible handwriting. It's ok to make him re-do things like this. I think he needs to slow down. I can tell he's rushing. Mr. Maple (Eric's tutor) also talked to Eric about being messy, so maybe if you say something, too, he'll get the message.

Thanks!

Rhonda V.

Eric's attention also was lacking, and a couple of weeks later, Mrs. Johnston wrote me the following note:

Mrs. Vardeman,

I haven't seen much improvement with his attention span & handwriting. He's still rushing & I'm having to stay on him to keep him focusing in class. He's still asking if he "has to do this." We have also started a class novel study of Little House on The Prairie. *He had told me that he can't understand unless it is read to him, but he can recall down to the last degree everything about his Goosebumps books. I'm not sure what direction I should take now. I do think his medicine dose should be looked at again. I just feel him slipping very quickly and I need some direction. Our inclusion teacher is only with him for reading on Mondays. If I need to send reading things home, I will. He seems to convey to me that he doesn't have to do reading assignments in class because he can do them at home. If you need to meet with me, please feel free to call. I'll be happy to do whatever I can to help.*

Thanks,

Mrs. Johnston

It became clear that Eric had begun to use the excuse of my working with him at home and Mr. Maple's working with him at tutoring to try to get out of doing his class work at school. He didn't get very far with that plan. I was spending so much time preparing study guides and working on reading with Eric each day that I was not willing to spend time with him going over work he was supposed to be doing in class. The students were given a good bit of freedom in the loosely structured classroom, and Eric was spending a lot of time drawing cartoon characters and monsters, all with tails.

I met with Mrs. Becken, Eric's principal, to discuss the problems he was having at school. I told her his focusing was off because of classroom distractions. He was not motivated and was becoming a behavior problem. He needs a structured classroom setting, I told her. We discussed whether it would be beneficial to move Eric back to the schedule he had the first half of the year where he would change classes. However, it was so far into the second semester, Mrs. Becken felt it would make the situation worse for him to make the change at that time. I understood and agreed, knowing that Eric didn't need any dramatic changes.

We had all been through a stressful first of the year. My dad, Curtis Jones, died in January of sepsis, a complication of pneumonia, at age 89. Although there was an age difference of 80 years between my dad and Eric, they had a good relationship. My dad, known as "Papa Bear" to his grandchildren, liked to tease the kids by using the wrong words and having them correct him. One afternoon, Eric was visiting my parents, and across the street from their home in Blanchard, a crew was clearing land for a new library. My dad told Eric to look out the window and see the big "hoeback." Eric looked and then quickly informed his grandfather that the machine was a "backhoe" and not a "hoeback." My dad roared with laughter.

Eric and his brother, Kurt, reacted to the news of their grandfather's death differently. Five-year-old Kurt began asking why the antibiotics given to my dad in the hospital didn't work. Eric just cried and cried. At the funeral home before the funeral began, Eric picked up an "In Memory" card for Gideon Memorial Bibles and filled in the "In Memory Of" with "Papa Bear" and wrote, "Don't forget that he is safe in heaven." He gave the card to my mother, who thought it was a very sweet gesture and saved it. He also told his grandmother that Papa Bear was his guardian angel.

At our May appointment with Dr. Horton, I explained how there were periods of time when we would lose Eric temporarily. He wasn't motivated at school, at home or at tutoring. I believed it was not medicine-related but was more of an attitude problem. I explained that his class at school was not structured, and I believed the change in Eric was chiefly caused by a lack of structure.

Dr. Horton gave me some teacher report forms to be filled out and told me to ask Mr. Maple if he noticed any difference in Eric's concentration at tutoring due to a slight increase in his medication that she had changed in December.

Dr. Horton noticed that Eric was squirming in the clinic, acted sleepy and was lying on her couch but exhibited no tics and his mood was euthymic, or normal.

Mr. Maple had completed a progress report that compared Eric's August 1999 Reading Center test to his current performance. The results were indicative of some great progress:

August 7, 1999		May 30, 2000	
Silent Reading Test			
Vocabulary	2.6 grade level 11%tile	3.9 grade level 30%tile
Comprehension	2.5 grade level 22%tile	4.5 grade level 45%tile
Total	2.6 grade level 16%tile	4.3 grade level 39%tile
Sight Word Vocab.	4.9 grade level 55%tile	8.5 grade level 95%tile

The report said Eric had made "outstanding progress during his tutoring sessions. He is a very cooperative student who works hard to focus on his assignments." Continued tutoring was recommended.

We talked to Dr. Horton about the upcoming summer months, and I reported Eric would continue gymnastics, and we had signed him up for art lessons. Eric had shown an interest in art, and we thought he might as well put all that drawing and coloring to good use. And maybe the art teacher could get him focused on something other than monsters.

Chapter Eleven

The Fifth Grade, Bullies and Reports

The summer of 2000 found us back at Gulf Shores in June with Rob's parents. Eric had a new summer haircut and spent a lot of time on the sand and in the gulf. He took art lessons and painted some beautiful still life pictures. At home, movies he watched inspired what characters he would draw. We started his tutoring back the week before school began.

At our August appointment with Dr. Horton, I asked the psychiatrist about a new drug I had heard about that would have the same effect as Ritalin but would last all day. Dr. Horton said Concerta, a sustained-release drug, was still in the testing stage and was not on the market at that time. It would be a few years before Dr. Horton would replace Eric's Ritalin with the non-stimulant drug Strattera that he would take once a day. The benefit of a drug like Strattera is the patient doesn't have the problem of the medicine's wearing off before the next dose is taken and starts working.

We had discontinued his Ritalin dosage during the summer, and Dr. Horton suggested we start him back on it. She told us to watch for indications of Eric's becoming listless or lethargic and to watch his appetite and weight. There were no tics observed while we were at the appointment, and I reported there were none at home.

The teacher report forms that Dr. Horton had given to me at the previous appointment in May were returned to her completed by Eric's teachers. The teachers reported they observed significant symptoms at the end of the school year.

Eric had started to school in August before our Dr. Horton appointment, and I reported that Eric had his four classes again with the same four teachers he had the first semester of his fourth-grade year. For maybe the first time in his life, he was showing some concern about what his peers thought of him. He was to gather four items to take to school that showed something about himself. I suggested his character cutouts for one of the items, and he didn't want to take them because he didn't want it to look like he played with "paper dolls." He also had been drawing some incredibly good head and neck portraits of people and animals. He was not impressed with his talent, however, because sometimes I would find the pictures wrinkled up and lying on the floor of his room.

I reported he had been doing some pacing if he was bored but it was fairly easy to get him out of it. Occasionally he was getting "stuck" on activities, but he could be redirected fairly easily. Also, he and Kurt had gotten along well during the summer. I told Dr. Horton we were beginning to research middle schools for the next fall when Eric would be entering the sixth grade. We had resumed his tutoring the week before school started, so we were hoping for a good academic year.

Eric was happy to be changing classes again at school, and because he had the same four teachers from his previous year, we didn't schedule a conference the first week of school.

Shortly after school started, Eric wrote a story about a dog. Although the story was titled, "Lucy," our dog's name, it was about a bull terrier named Jed.

One day when I came home from school my mother was waiting for me. She said we were going to a pet shop to get a dog. She drove her car to the pet shop. We walked inside. We saw a lot of dogs. We picked out a boy dog. We paid for him and drove home. On the way home I asked my mom if our dog would live a long time. She said "If you take good care of it and give it food and water it might." We named our dog Jed. He was a boy bull terrieir. He was kept inside the house sometimes, most of the time was outside. But the dog wasn't very friendly. He was a mean dog. He tore up the house a lot.

After reading Eric's story, I was glad we had Lucy, our Fox Terrier, who is a good little dog and definitely not a mean one.

As a fifth-grade student, Eric participated in D.A.R.E., an anti-drug program for children. One of the first things he did after attending one of the assemblies was draw a side view of a scary-looking character with spots on his face and his tongue hanging out. At the top, Eric had written the words, "Don't take drugs."

I continued to work with Eric at home, developing study guides and quizzing him in preparation for tests. We spent a lot of time reading and discussing the book, *Roll of Thunder, Hear My Cry* by Mildred D. Taylor, one of the first books the class was assigned to read. A story of racial injustice in the South, the book intrigued Eric so much we bought the movie, and he watched it several times. He also drew pictures of the characters in scenes from the book.

In October, we saw Dr. Horton, and I reported Eric had been hyper in the evenings, so we were leaving off his afternoon dose of Ritalin. During math, the last period at school, Eric was fidgeting a lot, but he was doing fine otherwise.

Rob and I told Dr. Horton that we noticed a vocal tic that previously had not been observed. Dr. Horton explained that Ritalin is known to worsen tics; however, we chose to continue the medication. We struggled with knowing what to do—not wanting Eric to have tics but knowing he needed the medication for his ADHD.

I also reported that we had selected a middle school for Eric—University Christian Prep (UCP)—which previously was known as Trinity Heights Christian Academy (THCA), the same high school where I graduated. Rob and I had visited several middle schools and thought UCP would meet Eric's needs academically as well as spiritually. We had met with the school's headmaster, Dr. Billy McCormack, who had been the headmaster at THCA when I was a student. We told Dr. McCormack about Eric and the challenges he faced having Asperger's Syndrome. We told him that Eric was mainstreamed in all classes even though he had a special education classification with modifications in the public school system. His grades were good, we explained, but abstract thinking was hard for him. As an example, I told him about a written problem Eric had in math that contained the words, "hockey division." Eric saw the word "division" and thought he needed to divide to get the answer. Dr. McCormack said the school was not only a "teaching place" but was a ministry with teachers who were focused on each student's needs, no matter what those needs are. Smaller classes than what Eric was accustomed to would provide for more individual attention for students.

In the fall of his fifth-grade year, Eric, who took his lunch to school every day, began giving most of his food away to a couple of boys in his class. We were not aware of it until I received a phone call from one of his teachers who said that Eric did not have a lunch that day and wanted to know if she could buy his lunch. She said all students either had to buy a lunch or bring a lunch, and he didn't have lunch money nor did he have anything to eat. I told her he had left home with a lunch, and I would find out what happened to it. After questioning Eric that afternoon, he said "Bobby" (not his real name) told him he would be Eric's friend if he would hand over his lunch. Apparently Eric thought the sacrifice was worth it. Of course, we tried to explain to him that true friends would not ask you to give up your lunch every day and he had to have a lunch at school. Those were the rules. Students were not to give away their lunches nor were they allowed to trade food. Although Eric was a stickler for following the rules, he wanted so badly to have friends. His main meal of the day was breakfast, so he was never very hungry at lunchtime anyway.

After finding out that Eric had been giving away most if not all of his lunch for several days, the teacher who let Eric borrow the lunch money ordered Bobby and another student to write notes to Eric apologizing for taking his lunch. The contents of the notes are below. The names of both students have been changed.

Eric,

I am sorry for saying that a couple of weeks ago. I told you I was just kidding and that you didn't have to give them to me any more. You just kept giving me them thinking I really meant that.

Bobby

To: Eric

I apoligize for takeing your snack after you gave it to me.

Tommy

The lunch issue was the first of many incidents involving Eric's bad judgment or peers taking advantage of him. There were several times when Eric was bullied by Bobby, and the behavior carried over into middle school.

One afternoon when Eric had taken all he could handle of Bobby's teasing, he took matters into his own hands. I was inside our house and had heard the school bus stop near our road. I didn't hear our carport door shut a few minutes later and wondered why Eric hadn't come inside. I opened the door, looked out, and lying on top of his backpack was a note:

Mother,

I've gone to beat up Bobby.

Love,

Eric

He had ridden his bicycle down the street to a neighbor's house where Bobby had been staying after school. I avoided the temptation to get in the car and drive to the house but decided to let Eric handle this one on his own. Kurt took off on his bike and arrived at the scene to find Eric and Bobby in a shouting match. Within a few minutes, both Eric and Kurt came home. I don't think Eric threw any punches at Bobby, but he was tired of the constant teasing and felt he had to do something about it.

At our January 2001 appointment with Dr. Horton, I told her about Eric's run-ins with Bobby but that Eric had written in his journal that week he wanted to invite Bobby to his birthday party. It was hard to understand, but I think Eric wanted to be everyone's friend and he easily forgave Bobby for being mean to him.

We reported that even though socially Eric was experiencing some problems, he was making good grades and was on task with his studies. As he had done each previous year of elementary school, Eric earned certificates for good grades and perfect attendance for the various nine-week grading periods.

Eric's special education progress report completed by Mrs. Thomas in December was filled with scores of "3's" which meant "greatly improved." She also had checked off "Puts forth effort," "Good attitude," "Well behaved" and "Follows classroom/school rules." The social objectives included "improve interpersonal skills" and "respect and understand personal rights of others."

There were a couple of issues we discussed with Dr. Horton: Eric seemed to be "stuck" on the computer game "Who Wants To Be A Millionaire," and he had exhibited some destructive behavior. My parents' home had a shed behind it, and Eric found that if he pulled on some loose panels, he could take them off. He had pulled off several panels before my mother discovered what he was doing and told him to stop. Later he said he knew he shouldn't have done that, but he couldn't stop. Dr. Horton told us to give him his allowance but then make him give it back to us when he did something he knew was wrong.

Eric's IEP was done on January 24, and I attended the meeting with the school and parish representatives.

Eric's strengths were listed in the following paragraph: *Eric has strong rote memory skills while application skills may vary. Reading comprehension is good due to sight vocabulary. Context and picture clues are not always used. Multiplication facts are mastered. Math calculation skills are also a strength.*

Support needs: *Eric has difficulty with questions requiring short-term auditory memory and similarities/differences. Difficulties are also recognized in developing interpersonal relationships and comprehending others' feelings, jokes, sarcasms. Change brings distress.*

Concerns of the parent: *Mrs. Vardeman has been very pleased with Eric's progress thus far in elementary school. However, as parents, they feel the best environment for middle school will be in a private setting.*

Evaluation results: *Eric has been successful with 504 accommodations since 2/99; however, interventions began much earlier. Problems remained with transitions, his rushing through tasks, need for reassurance that unfinished work can be done later and his not asking for help. Special ed services (inclusion) have been received since 01/00 and proven successful.*

Progress in general ed curriculum: *First nine wks GPA = 3.6; Second nine wks GPA = 3.8. Currently Eric has an A in all subjects. Study guides are provided for all tests and used effectively. Eric is a model student, obeying teacher directions and meeting all expectations.*

Statewide assessment results: *4th-grade LEAP results show weaknesses (below 30%) in Science as Inquiry, Science & the Environment, Measurement, Probability & Discrete Math, History and Locate, select & synthesize information. 100% scored in Read, analyze & respond and Algebra. Approaching basic on all tests except Science, which was unsatisfactory.*

Under the accommodations needed for LEAP testing, the IEP report listed the same accommodations that his 4th-grade IEP listed: *Tests read aloud except Reading Comprehension, Extended Time, Repeated Directions and Individual/Small Group.*

Eric's measurable short-term objectives for his 5th-grade IEP were geared more toward social interaction than toward academics. The four short-term goals were:

113

Given instruction, Eric will demonstrate improved interpersonal communication skills.

Given instruction, Eric will verbalize feelings toward peers in an appropriate manner.

Given instruction, Eric will understand and respect the personal rights of others.

Eric will complete a story web or similar strategy to identify key points in a specific text.

On March 1, we received a progress report from The Reading Center that said Eric "has continued to make outstanding progress as indicated by his report card." He had made "A's" in reading, math, language development and social studies with a "B" in science. Continued one-on-one tutoring was recommended with the focus of future sessions being on homework support with an emphasis on vocabulary and comprehension development.

Eric took the Iowa Test of Basic Skills in the spring of 2001, and the test results were much like those of other standardized tests he had taken. He scored higher in his strong areas of language arts and using reference materials and lower in reading comprehension and some areas of math such as probability and statistics.

The boys celebrated their 11th and 7th birthdays with a big family party at home on March 14 and with friends a couple of days later eating pizza and having a sleepover.

We took a trip during spring break to Houston where we visited NASA, taking a tour and viewing historical crafts such as Apollo 17. Eric had a great time practicing his "moon jump," a device where he was seated and strapped in and experienced semi-weightlessness. We also spent a few hours at the Houston zoo, an environment where Eric always was comfortable.

On Easter Sunday, April 15, Eric publically reaffirmed his baptism in church and was confirmed. He had participated with four other students in a confirmation class taught by our pastor, the Rev. Humphreys.   Eric had been baptized on Easter Sunday in 1990, a few weeks after he was born, so the confirmation's being on Easter Sunday held a special meaning for us. A photo of Eric, the other four students and the Rev. Humphreys shows Eric sandwiched in between the two girls in the class with his shoulders and arms drawn tightly toward the center of his body. Apparently the girls were a little too close for his comfort.

Chapter Twelve

"He Knows He's Different"

We were noticing increased hyperactivity with Eric during the month of April, and we decreased his Ritalin dose. He had done some strange things, such as biting his own arm as he pretended to be a snake. Also, he was continuing to act out things he was seeing in cartoons. The previous day, Eric had been playing with some neighborhood children near our home where there was a large mound of dirt. Eric challenged them to a dirt fight and ended up getting hit in the face with a stick. Apparently the other kids thought he wanted to fight.

"He doesn't mean any harm by it, but the other kids don't know that," I told Dr. Horton at our visit on April 21. "We need some pointers on how to help Eric socialize," I had written in my notes. She cautioned us about Eric's exposure to television and video and urged us to make sure he watches non-aggressive shows and movies. "When Eric is inappropriately aggressive, he needs consequences that are immediate, intense and short in duration," she said. She also told us to stop his Ritalin dose in the mornings. Dr. Horton noticed that Eric was blinking his eyes a lot at the appointment and asked him about it. He told her he was unaware he was doing it.

The psychiatrist recommended we call Dr. Perry Hill, a child psychologist, to have a behavioral assessment done. Also, she recommended Laurie Nussbaum, a licensed clinical social worker, who could do behavioral management therapy for Eric. It would be four years before we took Eric to an appointment with Mrs. Nussbaum, but he saw Dr. Hill two days later. Rob and I described Eric's problems of not relating to his peer group and how he would act out fantasy in real life. Dr. Hill also visited with Eric and gathered information. He found out something that we had never discussed with our oldest son. "He knows he's different (from his peers)," Dr. Hill said, "but he's ok with it."

We had several appointments during the spring and summer of 2001 with Dr. Hill, who worked with Eric to help him in four areas:

Meeting new people

Initiating play with others

Introducing himself into play and

Responding when others come to play.

His goals were to help Eric be more effective in peer relationships and to motivate him to come up with ideas for play. He talked with Eric about the definition of a friend and what friends do together socially. He also suggested that we role-play at home so Eric could practice these techniques. He encouraged us to educate Eric on Asperger's Syndrome so he could begin to feel more comfortable with himself.

Mrs. Thomas, the inclusion teacher, sent me a note on April 25 that said Eric's attentiveness and concentration ability has "drastically decreased with the absence of his Rx, but the reason is understood." The good news in her note was that a Caddo Parish speech therapist made visits to University Christian Prep, the middle school that we had chosen for Eric. He had qualified for speech therapy and had been seeing a speech therapist at Blanchard Elementary. With a speech therapist's going to UCP, Eric would be able to continue his IEP and classroom accommodations.

On April 27, I called Dr. Horton to report on Eric's progress with the decreased Ritalin. I told her I had started giving him a small amount of Ritalin in the mornings in addition to his noon dose because "he totally could not work at school without it." Dr. Horton reviewed with me the risks of the tics being worse with the stimulant, but until school was out, I didn't want to try a different medication. She urged us to continue to see Dr. Hill for behavior management of Eric's ADHD.

Eric's strong desire to have friends and to please them got him in trouble the next week. Another student told Eric if he would touch a girl's rear end, he would be Eric's friend. Eric did it, and he was assigned to in-school suspension (ISS). The principal, Mrs. Becken, called to tell me what happened and said that a report would be sent home describing the incident.

On the one hand, it was hard for me to believe Eric had done something he knew was wrong and was against the rules. On the other hand, I knew Eric wanted so badly to have friends that he would stoop to their demands. I was sad for Eric but upset with him and even more upset with the kids at school who found pleasure in dangling Eric from a string like a puppet.

Even though the school was punishing Eric for "being disrespectful toward a student," I felt he needed to know how serious the incident was, and I invoked punishment at home. I typed out his punishment and had Rob, myself and Eric sign it:

Eric will not be allowed to play outside before or after school through Friday, May 4, 2001.

Eric will not be able to keep the new video "MVP."

Eric will not earn an allowance for two weeks.

Eric will not be allowed computer time though Friday, May 4, 2001.

Eric didn't like being stuck inside the classroom all day, and we hoped this meant he had learned his lesson and wouldn't buckle to peer pressure.

A few days later Mrs. Becken called me and said one of Eric's teachers had filled out a behavior report on Eric, and he would be bringing the report home that day. My heart sank. What had he done now? The report said Eric was asked to stay in his seat until she could help him. "He did not follow directions," the report said. Mrs. Becken gave me the option of delaying Eric's punishment of having to sit in the office until after the Field Day carnival that fell on the next day. I told her Eric needed to suffer the consequences and miss Field Day. I didn't want him to receive preferential treatment, and also I believed the sooner the punishment was given, the better.

I wasn't sure if Eric was unable to stay in his seat because of the lack of Ritalin or if he was going through a phase, but the incidents at school were frustrating to me and I was ready to see some behavior improvements.

Eric ended the school year with perfect attendance, good grades and several awards including a Principal's Honor Roll trophy. Even though he had gotten into a little trouble during the last month of school, he was more outgoing and seemed to be better adjusted socially. Our visits with Dr. Hill were continuing, and the psychologist helped Eric greatly in that area. But there were still issues to be faced.

On June 9, we saw Dr. Horton, and I reported that Eric had been pacing, he was easy to "fly off the handle" and he couldn't be still. His current obsession was the radio and radio station settings. Dr. Horton suggested trying a different medication—Clonidine—to replace his Ritalin dosage. Clonidine is used to treat ADHD and Tourette's, in addition to other uses such as controlling high blood pressure. Dr. Horton thought the Clonidine might help control Eric's impulsivity, eye blinking and pacing. He also was making a noise in his throat that was either a tic, sinus trouble or a habit. In addition to the Clonidine-Ritalin change, Dr. Horton increased his Prozac dosage. Eric weighed 74 pounds, and he had outgrown his current dosage. We were to watch for side effects of Clonidine, which were drowsiness and an increased appetite.

When we returned to see Dr. Horton in July, Eric was still agitated, restless and impulsive. He had been asking us time after time questions about certain songs and had been very talkative at home. We reported Eric had been sleepy after taking the Clonidine and he had fallen asleep at his Dr. Hill appointment. I told Dr. Horton I was not opposed to the Clonidine, but I felt he needed to get more adjusted to it before school started in the fall.

If Eric stayed on the Clonidine, he couldn't take Ritalin, which worked better for his ADHD. With Clonidine's being more effective for Tourette's, Dr. Horton wanted to find out if Eric actually had Tourette's or if his tics were merely habits. She wanted us to take Eric to see Dr. James Kim, a neurologist, to have an electroencephalogram (EEG), a test measuring the electrical activity of the brain. We needed to know his opinion on whether to continue a psychostimulant such as Ritalin or whether Eric would be better served taking Clonidine. All I knew was it was time to do some heartfelt praying that Eric's didn't have Tourette's, but if he did, I needed to have the strength to handle it.

Chapter Thirteen

An EEG and a New School

On July 19, Eric had all sorts of wires hooked up to his head from the EEG machine, and while he was fascinated with the experience, I was blinking back tears. It wasn't easy seeing my son lying on a hospital bed with wires attached to his head. I suppose in the back of my mind, I also was worried Eric might have a brain tumor. I mentioned to Dr. Kim his occasional headaches that occurred usually after swimming. He put my mind at ease.

When the results of the EEG came back, we were relieved to find out everything was normal. It was determined Eric's eye blinking and other repetitive behaviors were merely habits and not Tourette's. These results were good news and another answer to prayer. We were told to keep an eye out for a change in Eric's patterns and not to bring attention to the repetitive habits. That was so much easier to do than deal with the alternative—adjusting to Tourette's. Also, Eric would no longer take Clonidine because we knew for certain he didn't have Tourette's.

We kept Eric busy working in the yard at home during the summer when he wasn't taking art lessons or swimming on a local swim team. One yard project he worked on with his dad was installing a brick patio. He enjoyed the task because he was putting the bricks in a specific pattern. This was repetitive behavior that was all right and even expected.

In August, our family went to Six Flags Over Texas in Arlington for a mini-vacation before school started. There was no ride too scary for our fearless older son, and he rode several roller coasters, including the Titan, a new roller coaster climbing more than 225 feet high with a top travel speed of 85 mph. If the lines hadn't been so long, he probably would have ridden the Titan several times.

Rob and I met with Dr. Hill on August 13, and he gave us a couple of things to work on with Eric. He suggested working on conversational skills and encouraging Eric to maintain the topic being discussed. In order to establish deeper friendships and share personal information, normal interactions would help with that, he said. The other area was practicing and applying the skills of problem-solving. Repetitiveness is needed, even basic repetitiveness, such as saying "goodbye" to people, Dr. Hill explained. He said to find natural opportunities to show things to Eric and translate them into short-term goals. For example, if Eric wants more friends on the playground, he should set a goal for the next day or two. During recess, spend time with the children outside, and decide who to talk to, what to say and when to do it. If something went wrong, decide what to do differently next time. Eric could use these strategies at his new school that he would begin in a few days. These were all great ideas we began using.

Eric's first day of middle school at University Christian Prep was August 20, and this was the first time he had to wear a uniform to school, something I was grateful for because there were no decisions to be made on school attire each day. Eric looked grown up in his pin-striped blue and white shirt, navy pants, black belt and black dress shoes.

Soon after school started, Rob and I met with Eric's teachers just as we had done in elementary school to give them some background information on him. His classes were art humanities, math, English, reading, social studies, science and P.E./health. He had the same teacher for English and reading and for social studies and science. He also had an introduction to Greek and Latin that was incorporated into his English class. Most of the teachers commented they had not noticed Eric was different in any way. We were very happy to hear that news. The teachers all said they were willing to help Eric and accommodate his needs as best they could. The sixth grade class was small—only 17 students—and we knew Eric could get more individual attention.

On August 29, I met with school representatives and Jo Linn Burt, the speech therapist assigned to UCP, for a Services Plan for Eric's school year. Eric and I both attended the meeting as well as the school's principal, a teacher and Ms. Burt. The plan outlined objectives for the school year but first gave the following general student information:

Strengths: rote memory and math calculation skills. Weaknesses: short-term auditory memory, social language skills, higher-order problem solving. Modifications/accommodations needed for distractibility and difficulties with abstract reasoning and organizational skills. Evaluation revealed mild-moderate language delay. Specialized equipment: none needed at this time. Health needs: medical dx of Asperger's Syndrome and obsessive compulsive disorder, takes medication daily and under care of Dr. Rita Horton. Vision and hearing WFL. He also has allergies—is on medication. Transitional needs: none due to age. Eric is performing on grade level with assistance. Special factors: due to Asperger's Syndrome often misinterprets instructions. Communication needs: requires Speech-Language Pathology Services for difficulties in abstract reasoning, social language and organizational skills. Statewide assessment results: 4th-grade LEAP Approaching Basic in all areas but Science, which was unsatisfactory. Parent feels Eric has made good progress but feels he continues to require Speech Language Pathology Services.

Under "Service Needs," Communication was selected out of the other categories of Academic/Cognitive, Motor, Behavior, Self-Help, Social and Vocational.

The Specific Current Performance area had the following: *Eric passed all subjects last year on or above grade level with support from inclusion teacher and Speech Language Pathologist. He met objectives to verbalize feelings to peers appropriately and to understand and respect the personal rights of others. Due to a mild-moderate language delay, characterized by difficulties in social language skills, abstract thinking skills and organizational skills, Eric needs support from Speech Language Pathology Services.*

The annual goal: *Eric will increase social language skills, abstract reasoning skills and problem solving.*

The method of measurement would be through Speech Language Pathologist/Teacher observation and assessment data.

The following were listed as Measurable Short-Term Objectives/Benchmarks:

Eric will answer higher level comprehension questions requiring inference, cause-effect and predicting at 80% accuracy 3 of 4 sessions.

Eric will maintain topic during conversation for 7 mins. in 3 of 4 sessions.

Eric will interpret American English idioms accurately at 80% 3 of 4

sessions.

Eric will interpret body language/facial expressions accurately at 80% 3 of 4 sessions.

Eric will answer problem-solving questions at 80% accuracy 3 of 4 sessions.

Eric will reduce the number of questions he asks during conversation from 10 to 5 in a 15-min. conversation 3 of 4 sessions.

The special education services would be twice a week for 30 minutes each, with one session in the classroom and one session out of the classroom, one-on-one with Ms. Burt.

The report reinforced Eric's need for classroom accommodations and referred to his previous 504 IEP in the public school. Under "Supports for School Personnel" was the statement, "Classroom teachers will be educated on accommodations needed for success in classroom."

The following month, Eric's yearly evaluation was done. Referred to as an IAP in private school, the following accommodations were listed:

Assign preferential seating

Use notebook for assignments/materials/homework

Provide individualized/small group instructions

Reduce/minimize distractions

Stand near student when giving directions

Modify assignments as needed (vary length, limit items)

Break tasks and procedures into sequential steps

Teach concrete concepts before teaching abstract concepts

Modify/repeat/model directions

Limit amount of work required

Provide instruction in social skills.

One testing accommodation was listed: *Give tests in smaller portions.*

At our Dr. Horton appointment on September 8, the psychiatrist noticed Eric was blinking his eyes repeatedly, and apparently he had been doing that at school because his art teacher suggested he might need glasses. He had been asking Rob and me a lot of questions about a rock band, so he was still having some OCD symptoms. Even though he was not having the severe OCD symptoms he had when he was little, Eric continued to "get stuck" on various subjects, and it seemed each time we had a Dr. Horton appointment, he was fixated on a different topic.

Chapter Fourteen

September 11, 2001, and Sixth Grade

On September 11, 2001, I was working part-time for the Rev. Frances Attaway in her ministry office. She is the minister who had prayed for Eric when he was younger. Shortly after 9 a.m., Rob, who was working as an engineer for a local TV station, called and told me two airliners had crashed into the World Trade Center's twin towers in New York City a few minutes apart. Later known as 9/11, the terrorist attack on America was the worst disaster in our nation's history. I remember feeling worried and scared that the four planes that crashed were only the beginning of an attack on the United States.

I wanted to pick up my boys from school and make sure they were safe. I turned on a TV at the ministry office and monitored the national news story on the attack and listened as local news break-ins urged parents not to take their children out of school. The airports were closed and no flights were taking off, but I heard what must have been Air Force One fly overhead taking President George W. Bush to Barksdale Air Force Base in Bossier City, just over the river from Shreveport. By the time I picked up both boys that afternoon, they had learned of the attack and had what seemed like thousands of questions.

A few days later, one of Eric's assignments was to write a paper on what had happened on Sept. 11. He wrote:

World Trade Center Attack

On Sept. 11, 2001, terrorists attacked America. Two hijacked planes were crashed into the World Trade Centers. One plane crashed into the Pentagon and other crashed in Pennsylvania. We think the last plane was aiming for the White House, but some of the passengers may have forced them to crash in Pennsylvania. Both the World Trade Center towers later fell down. More than five thousand people were killed in the attack. All of the airports were closed for safety.

President George Bush flew here to Barksdale Air Force Base to make a speech. Later he went home to Washington, D.C.

Osama Bin Laden may have hired the terrorists to do it. He told them if you do this you will go to heaven. That was a lie. They don't know for sure that Bin Laden is guilty. We won't bomb him and his people until we are sure. The terrorists didn't like the United States helping Israel and they wanted to get back at us.

It might become a war, World War III, but I hope not. For now we will keep praying for all the victims and their families.

For a sixth-grader who sometimes had a difficult time putting his thoughts into words, Eric had a good understanding of what had happened, and he was absolutely right about the urgent need for prayer.

As our nation struggled to deal with the tragedy of 9/11, Rob and I, as parents, were trying to keep things as normal as possible at home so our children would not be afraid to go to school, church and other activities. Time went on and we had to continue our lives.

A couple of weekends later, Rob took Eric and Kurt fishing at Toledo Bend Lake in Sabine Parish near Many, Louisiana. After a day of fishing, they went swimming, and Eric stepped on a piece of glass in the lake, cutting a gash in his foot. They drove home, dropped off Kurt, and Rob took Eric to the emergency room of a nearby hospital. A few hours later, they came home, Eric on crutches. He was to keep weight off his foot for a week. He hobbled around at school on the crutches but had plenty of attention from his female classmates, who carried his books and helped him get around.

A few weeks after school started, Dr. Horton gave me teacher evaluations for Eric's teachers to complete. Some of his teachers observed Eric had difficulty sustaining attention; he fidgeted or squirmed in his seat and was easily distracted. Karen

Whitehead, Eric's science and social studies teacher, wrote:

Eric is a very intelligent student. He is doing well on his exams. It's just at times he has difficulty concentrating on a particular task at hand. However, he is very nice and respectful.

Eric's reading/English teacher, Janna Bellar, witnessed a few more problems:

Eric seems to be struggling with following through with directions. I have also noticed an increase in his making noises during class. One thing that concerns me is his willingness to do what other classmates tell him to without his ever questioning or thinking about the consequences.

These were issues we worried about as well and constantly discussed with Eric. Even though sometimes Eric's attention was not good, he scored well on tests and made all "A's" and "B's" on his first two six weeks report cards.

Never one to like to write in cursive, Eric was encouraged, however, to abandon his favorite way of writing—printing in block letters—and to do his writing in cursive. On one of his spelling tests, Eric printed the first four words and then switched to cursive for the remainder of the test. Apparently unsure of his skill in cursive writing, he printed two of the words and then wrote at the top of the page, "I thought you couldn't read some so I wrote them in print beside the two words."

Eric enjoyed his art humanities class and continued his love for drawing people and animals during his sixth-grade year. He sketched Garfield the cat, John Lennon, Paul McCartney and George Harrison of the Beatles, and the subject of J.K. Rowling's books and later popular movies, Harry Potter. He had a knack for seeing a characteristic of the person he was drawing and transferring that to paper. For instance, the big eyes and round glasses of Harry Potter.

He also liked his math teacher, Kathleen Robinson, and wrote on the top of his homework paper, "You're the best math teacher I know." Underneath Eric's words, Mrs. Robinson wrote,

"You're the best Eric I know." On another homework assignment, Eric wrote, "I love you, Mrs. Robinson." She wrote, "Thank you. I need that!"

Ms. Burt, the speech teacher, continued to work with Eric two days a week to meet his IAP objectives. She worked with him on communication and language with inference and idioms. On a special education progress report, Eric scored a "2" or "improving" on inference and a "3" on idioms. Ms. Burt wrote, "Greatly improved in understanding of idioms." With Eric's literal interpretation of most everything, his understanding of idioms was a huge "step in the right direction." All his life, Eric had seen things concretely as either black or white with little or no comprehension of gray areas. Ms. Burt helped Eric understand gray areas.

We were very pleased with all of Eric's teachers, and they encouraged him by putting smiley faces and writing "very good" on several of his papers. On a social studies test, he made a 98%, and the teacher wrote, "Eric had 2nd highest grade." All of these comments and good grades helped build Eric's self-confidence, and he loved school. It also helped him socially because he made several new friends. He began liking a fifth-grader, Dixie Moses, a cute blonde curly-haired girl with whom he had been in the same Mother's Day Out group when he was very young. They were so young they didn't remember each other from long ago, but they developed a friendship that would last several years. Eric's way of expressing he liked Dixie might have been a little different from the approach of other boys his age: He liked to hide in the bushes and jump out and surprise her. She thought he was funny, and he didn't care that no one else approached a girl like that. They had several dates at the skating rink, attended some carnivals and visited in each other's homes.

Eric also met Stinson Bundrick, who would be his best friend through middle school, high school and beyond.

We saw Dr. Horton in November, and Eric was still blinking his eyes, although she noted the blinking was not as "hard." I told her I felt that his blinking was more of a habit than a tic. Sometimes it seemed Eric was blinking his eyes more in front of Dr. Horton than he was anyone else. We wondered if it was because Dr. Horton asked about it and put the thought in his mind.

In February at our appointment with the psychiatrist, I reported Eric was doing well in school with his grades, and he was taking more responsibility for studying on his own. He was making friends and interacting more with other students. Also, I told her, Eric had done very well in a Bible Trivia game played with the youth group at church, probably because he had learned a lot of the information at school. Each class incorporated Christianity into the subject. In addition to his good grades and doing well socially, Eric's eye contact was better as was his ability to read emotions of other people. "This has been the best year Eric has had so far," I told Dr. Horton.

There were concerns, however, in May when we visited her. Eric had been misbehaving in class, not bringing his assignments notebook home or not completing it with homework assigned, and his grades were dropping. This seemed to be a pattern for Eric each spring. He was ready for school to be out and he fell into the "slacker" mode.

Another concern we had was that Eric had started doing some things at home that were destructive, such as pulling down the basketball goal that had started to lean. Also, he and Kurt, while trying to be helpful, had ruined the lawnmower by filling the gasoline compartment with used motor oil. They told me they were planning to surprise me by mowing the yard. I was more than surprised.

Dr. Horton noted Eric was blinking his eyes some but not as often as he has been. She wanted us to decrease his Ritalin dosage during the summer as usual. She reminded us that a low dose of Ritalin will help with Eric's attention, but if the dose is too high, it can create hyperactivity and nervousness. She suggested Eric spend a few minutes each day reviewing what was discussed in class to help prepare him for the next day. This task would help him even if he didn't write his homework assignments in his notebook.

At the end of his sixth-grade school year in 2002, Eric had made only three "C's" on his report card, the rest were "A's" and "B's," and by being on the honor roll, he was invited to attend the Honors Banquet in May.

The summer of 2002 was busy for Eric: He read novels that were assigned as homework over the summer for the next school year, went to church camp, took art lessons again and spent a lot of time swimming and going to Watertown, a Shreveport water park. Our family went to New Orleans on vacation in July, visiting relatives and friends, and visiting the Aquarium and the French Quarter and seeing the Mississippi River and Lake Pontchartrain.

We saw Dr. Horton on August 8, and the psychiatrist put Eric on a new medication for ADHD—Metadate. Unlike Ritalin that wears off after a few hours, Metadate releases an even dosage over several hours, lasting throughout the day. Dr. Horton noted Eric's obvious eye-blinking as well as a twitch in his left shoulder. We were hoping the new medication would decrease these repetitive habits. I probably depended too heavily on medication to fix Eric's problems and had to remind myself constantly that behavior modification was equally—if not more—important for treating Eric's symptoms.

Chapter Fifteen

"The Worst Day of My Life"

Eric started his seventh-grade year in August 2002 and had five different teachers for his seven classes: math, Bible, reading, language arts (English), life science, American history and health/P.E.

On August 27, he wrote his autobiography for English class:

It was a cool and windy day when my parents were going up to the hospital to have a baby named Eric. It was March 14, 1990, the day I was born. The doctor told Rob and Rhonda Vardeman (my parents) to come inside her office. She told them it was time to take me home. When I grew older my mom told me about the day I was born. She said that I was real fat and that I had three chins. Of course all that changed when I started losing weight. When I started going to daycare when I was about four, I started having more fun. I met new friends and had a good time. When I started school we started having assemblyies and I'd get certificates for doing well in school. At my new church, Lakeview United Methodist, I sang in the church programs. I have passed elementary school and in the seventh grade. When I grow up I hope to work at Johnny's Pizza House. I will try to help my child or children do well in school like I do.

It was interesting to note what parts of his life Eric chose to write about, but overall, it was a positive piece about having a good time, doing well in school, participating in church activities and looking toward the future. I was thankful Eric didn't write about the hard times and struggles in his life but was upbeat and positive.

Even though Eric was blinking his eyes and twitching his left shoulder, the tics had decreased by the time we had a

September appointment with Dr. Horton. She noted he was "very pleasant" in the clinic. We reported he had not experienced any side effects on the Metadate, and he was sleeping well. His appetite, although not decreased, was very limited in what he wanted to eat, something not unusual for our older son.

One afternoon when I picked Eric up from school, he got in the car and sighed. "This is the worst day of my life," he said. Bobby, the bully who had caused Eric so much grief in elementary school, had enrolled at UCP. The news put a damper on my day, too, although I tried to remain positive and encourage Eric not to let it get to him. There were some incidents in the weeks ahead, however, that were reflective of the old days back in elementary school. Bobby sat behind Eric in one class and wrote on his uniform shirt with a permanent marker. Also, he would prank call our house and leave weird messages on our answering machine. The next year, when Eric was in the 8th grade and had all he could take of Bobby and his mischievousness, he stood up, walked over and hit Bobby so hard, he knocked him out of his chair. Even though Eric probably should have been sent to the office for fighting, he didn't get in trouble. The other students as well as his teachers must have been as tired of Bobby's treatment of Eric as he was.

I had been in touch with Ms. Burt, the speech therapist, during the summer, and she sent a notice to me that Eric was due for a re-evaluation for his IEP. The date was scheduled for October 17. I was so thankful to have Ms. Burt working with Eric on speech and hearing therapy because not only was she making progress with Eric, but also she was helpful to me in making sure that the IAP was done each year. It was much harder to set up meetings and follow through with Eric's accommodation plan in a private school than it was in a public school. In the public school, the school initiates the IEP meetings, but for children in a private school, the task falls on the parents to ensure that the meetings are scheduled and held timely. The UCP teachers and administration were cooperative, but I had more responsibilities while Eric was there.

The Instructional/Environmental Accommodations on Eric's IAP were listed in a single paragragh:

Eric will be given preferential seating in the classroom which will be a limited number of students, preferably under 15. There will be conscious awareness of minimizing distractions in classroom during instruction and testing. There will be modified instructions as needed and concrete instructions over abstract. Eric will be given a notebook for assignments, and instructions in social skills will be attempted.

The re-evaluation listed information that had been reviewed, such as procedures for current exceptionalities, previous evaluation reports, classroom-based observation, standardized/school-based tests, parent information, medical diagnosis and performance in the general curriculum.

The report named Eric's primary exceptionality of Autism/Asperger's Syndrome and medical impairments of OCD, ADHD, Pervasive Developmental Disorder, chronic motor tics and allergies. The re-evaluation results were that Eric should continue to receive special education services and modifications. A part of the report was Eric's special education progress report, and Ms. Burt marked "3's" or greatly improved and wrote, "greatly improved with problem solving and interpreting idioms." She also checked off "puts forth effort," "good attitude" and "well behaved."

One class Eric enjoyed in his seventh-grade year was Bible, and he excelled in it. He had no problem memorizing the books of the Bible and Bible verses for tests. His teacher, Jason McInnis, sent me a nice note:

Mrs. Vardeman,

I just wanted to let you know that Eric made a 96% A on his test today. That, along with one other student, was the highest grade on this test. Eric is a joy to teach.

Jason McInnis

In November, Ms. Burt re-evaluated Eric and determined that he no longer met the criteria for speech services. Eric and I had mixed emotions over the news, because we both loved Ms. Burt and would miss having her work with Eric. The good news was she had done such a good job, Eric no longer needed to have the additional speech therapy. She wrote the following in her report:

Eric has been receiving speech services since 1999 for a mild-moderate language delay, characterized by weaknesses in problem solving, pragmatic skills and comprehension deficits. He has been working on problem solving, vocabulary comprehension, turn taking, topic maintenance, understanding of English idioms, higher level comprehension and other pragmatic/social skills. Eric met objectives to verbalize feelings toward peers in an appropriate manner, respect the personal rights of others, and to identify the key points in a specific text. He has also met objectives to maintain topic during conversation for 7 minutes, and to reduce the number of questions he asks during conversation from 10 to 5 in a 15-minute conversation. Eric has also greatly improved understanding of English idioms, answers higher level comprehension questions with greater accuracy and answers problem-solving questions with greatly improved accuracy.

Observations by the classroom teacher revealed Eric is functioning well in the classroom academically. She reports he is "slightly hesitant in oral responses" but otherwise she sees no special problems. Observations by the SLP revealed Eric was attentive, followed directions and was conscientious about completing tests and assignments.

A recent administration of the Comprehensive Assessment of Spoken Language revealed a total standard score of 81 placing Eric in the 99th percentile. His score for pragmatic judgment was lower than scores for other subtests, but his SS of 74 indicates only a mild delay which is expected for a child with his exceptionality and can be addressed in the classroom. He earned Standard Scores of 91 for Idiomatic Language and 92 for Nonliteral Language, indicating his comprehension of idioms was above what is expected for a student his age. Voice and fluency continue to be within acceptable limits. Eric no longer meets the criteria for speech impairment-language and is dismissed from speech.

With the common use of idioms in everyday language, it was important for Eric to understand these phrases that were not meant to be taken literally—phrases such as "That takes the cake" and "It's raining cats and dogs." Eric had made great progress by having had speech services, and Rob and I were thankful that he had "cleared another hurdle in his life."

Chapter Sixteen

Stinson

Eric spent a lot of time on the weekends with his friend, Stinson, either at Stinson's home in Bossier City or at our house. One of the interesting ways Eric related to the things going on in his life was to draw pictures or write about them. He wrote a story about Stinson—a fictional, somewhat humorous tale of meeting his school friend. He incorporated a couple of his favorites in the story: his favorite state—Maine—and his favorite color—green. The story was fairly long but contained only one paragraph.

My New Friend, Stinson

By Eric Vardeman

It was a beautiful summer morning in August as I was getting ready for my first day of school this year. My mom called for me to hurry up and get in her car. We lived up in Maine, where it was really cold almost all year round except for in the summer. I didn't realize it at first that we were already at my new school, Violet Jr. High. Like, I'd rather call it Violent Jr. High, because the kids here really start fights, the teachers are mean and you can almost get expelled every day. My name is Paul Green and you'd think I'm weird because I never really wanted to go to this school anyway. "Paul, you're wasting time, get out of the car," my mom yelled. I quickly got out of the car as my mom said goodbye to me. I hurried in the door as my mom drove away in her car. This school was enormous. I saw hallways, water fountains and zillions of classrooms. There were hundreds of kids, some about my age and some were as tall as trees. I saw that some were going into a big room. I tried to hurry up but two big guys, that were probably eighth graders, blocked my path into the big room that looked like a gym. "Where do you think you're going, little kid," one said. I said, "I thought we were supposed to go in here first." They both started cracking up. "Only eighth graders are allowed to come in

here, sixth and seventh graders go to the cafeteria down the hall,"
he pointed to a small room way down the hall. I started to say
thank you but I just wanted to get to the cafeteria. I started to run
down the hall toward the cafeteria when I slipped and cut my arm
on the side of the water fountain. Blood was starting to stain on
my short sleeve shirt. I tried to get up but I stayed in the same
position. A woman came rushing to help me, she was probably a
teacher. "What happened?" she asked in a screeching voice. "I
was running to the cafeteria when I slipped and cut my arm on the
side of the water fountain," I said. "Why were you running?" she
asked. "I thought I was late and I didn't know where I was
supposed to go." "You know running is not allowed in the
hallways," she said. "Now come with me, we'll get you an ice
pack." I followed her to the office and she got me an ice pack and
told me don't ever run in the cafeteria again and sent me on my
way. When I came to the cafeteria, I pushed the doors and went in,
everybody was staring at me. One kid said, "You're late, punk." I
ignored him and found a seat. I asked the boy next to me what his
name was. He said, "Stinson." I asked Stinson if he'd ever been
to this school before. He said this was his first year also. He said
he didn't really want to go to school here. Just when I was about
to say something the door opened and a man stepped in. "I am the
principal," he said. "Welcome to Violet Jr. High. At this time you
will proceed to your classrooms. When I call your grade you will
follow your teachers to your classrooms without talking. As we
walked down the hall, I noticed a classroom door knob that was
gone. "Maybe it was pulled off by one of the eight graders." We
walked and came past the office and into classroom 206. I sat
down in a seat next to Stinson. "'Paul Green," the teacher called.
"I need you to come sit here on the second row." "But I want to
sit by my new friend, Stinson." "Now" she yelled at me. I didn't
want to make things worse, so I just sat down where the teacher
told me to sit. "But how come I can't sit by Stinson," I
complained. "Because I said so," the teacher said. I just shut my
mouth. "Now class," the teacher said, "I am Mrs. Pepper, and I
will be your homeroom teacher for this year." "We don't switch
classes," I said. "Nah," one of the kids blurted out to me in my
face. "Quiet while I take roll," said Mrs. Pepper. I looked back at
the desk next to Stinson. It was empty. I quietly snuck back to sit

by Stinson when the teacher wasn't looking. A girl on the third row gave me a thumbs up. I whispered a question to Stinson and asked him how old he was. "I'm twelve," he said in a whisper. "Hey, me too," I said a little bit too loud. Mrs. Pepper turned and looked at me. "You're busted" said one kid. I told him to shut up and Mrs. Pepper sent me outside. As I stood out there I heard laughter coming from inside room 206. I stared at the old rusted walls in front of me not making a sound, waiting for Mrs. Pepper to come and let me back in the classroom. A few minutes later the classroom door swung open and Mrs. Pepper came rushing out. "Now if you can't keep your mouth shut and can't sit where you're supposed to then you can just have an automatic two-day suspension," Mrs. Pepper yelled. I can be really crazy sometimes but talk about her, she's crazier, I thought to myself. I came back in the classroom as quiet as a mouse and went to sit by Stinson. "Get up and come back to your assigned seat," Mrs. Pepper yelled. "Make me," I said, as I didn't know what I was saying as she came over to my desk. "What did you say," she asked in a terrifying tone of voice. "That wasn't me, that was him," I said in an embarrased voice. "No, it wasn't you liar," the other kid yelled at me. Noise started bursting from the classroom. "Quiet," said Mrs. Pepper. "Now, I don't know who said it but I know one thing if Paul doesn't get back in his seat right now, then he'll be taking a trip to a place called the office." I quickly got to my seat forgetting about Stinson. I glanced at the clock and saw that it was almost time to go home. The principal came on the intercom and said he would call us by grades and tell us where to wait for our parents to come pick us up. When he called "7th Grade," I rushed down the hall ignoring what that teacher told me about running. My mom came about ten minutes later. She asked how did my first day go. "Okay," I said not telling her about what happened. I told her about my new friend Stinson and asked if he could spend the night Friday. "Sure, if it's okay with his parents," my mom said, "Great, I have his phone number in my back pack, I'll call him when we get home. As soon as we got home I quickly called his parents and his dad said it would be fine. The week was passing by fast and I still didn't know everybody's names. I know a boy named John, two girls named Katy and Elizabeth, they were best friends, and I knew Stinson. Friday finally came, after school

Stinson's parents brought him over following the directions that my mom gave them. My mom and dad that just got home visited with Stinson's parents while we played cards. We had the greatest time, we watched movies, went to a basketball game and played chess. I'll never forget my new best friend "Stinson."

Without knowing anything about the conflicts in writing fiction short stories and books—man against man, man against nature, man against society and man against himself—Eric took conflict writing to a new level: Man (or in his case, boy) against mean teachers and school administration. In the story, Eric had to get accustomed to a new school, survive an injury, argue with teachers and endure bullying eighth-graders in order to form a friendship with Stinson. Although his story was purely fiction, I can't help but think how the struggles Eric had endured in his life were similar to his fictional story's efforts to befriend Stinson. And in both cases, it was worth the trouble.

Chapter Seventeen

A Teenager in the House

In December, we visited Dr. Horton and reported Eric was doing well on Metadate. However, there are some things that medicine doesn't cure. Eric was having some behavioral problems in class—giggling and making faces. The result of his immature behavior was having his desk turned around to face the wall and being sent out of class a couple of times. Rob decided to embarrass Eric by sitting in on one of the classes and had forewarned him he was going to do it. Eric kept asking Rob if he was kidding about sitting in on the class and was a little surprised when his dad showed up one day and sat in the back of the room. I told Dr. Horton Eric didn't misbehave as much after that, but the problems "are not completely gone." I also reported Eric had been upset when Bobby enrolled at UCP, and I had talked to the teachers and made them aware of past problems. Dr. Horton recommended Eric try new opportunities such as sports to give him something to occupy his mind when he wasn't studying.

Eric's current obsessive interest was movies and their ratings. This interest was something that would continue for years and came in handy when Eric worked in his dad's music store.

Eric's English teacher, Carmen Heflin, assigned a book report on *The Lion, The Witch and the Wardrobe* by C.S. Lewis. Eric enjoyed the book and earned an "A" on his report. His review part of the report follows:

This story is about a small closet known as a wardrobe that the children—Lucy, Edmund, Susan, and Peter—find in the Professor's house. The Professor is their godfather. The wardrobe has a secret passageway to the land of Narnia. The land is not known to the Professor, only to Edmund, Lucy, Susan, and Peter.

Lucy met a faun named Mr. Tumnus and became friends with him. Edmund met the Witch of Narnia who cast a spell that made it winter all the time. It was never Christmas or Spring in the land of Narnia. The witch even had some trees as spies who spied on the children. Later on Mr. Tumnus was captured by the wolves who were on the side of the witch.

Lucy helped rescue him with the aid of the Beavers and Aslan, the Great Lion. Aslan also helped Lucy and the other children get rid of the witch and save the forest.

I recommend this book because it is an exciting story.

* * * * *

Eric became a teenager on March 14, and we celebrated with a big family party at our house. I made invitations on the computer, and the front of the card had three pictures of Eric—as a baby, at age five with a big grin on his face and his eighth-grade spring picture. We decorated the dining room for the event and had a house full of relatives. I let Eric choose the menu, so he picked macaroni and cheese, fried chicken drummets, smoked sausage, chips, birthday cake, chocolate chip cookies and plenty of Dr. Pepper. I added finger sandwiches, a vegetable tray with Ranch dressing, queso dip, shrimp dip, peanut butter cookies and several different kinds of soft drinks. It was Kurt's birthday, too, so he had his own cake and a party on another day at a gymnastics center.

The next week, we went snow skiing in Santa Fe during spring break. Eric was more relaxed and did much better on the slopes during this trip than he did when he was nine and hyperventilated. Kurt had a better time on this trip, too, and learned to ski.

Rob took Eric to see Dr. Horton on April 12, and he reported to her that Eric had a good appetite, but the school was reporting an increase in negative behavior. Eric was laughing too much in class. Dr. Horton gave Rob an information booklet on the non-narcotic drug Strattera for us to consider for Eric's ADHD symptoms.

Eric's IAP was done in April 2003, and the plan was to continue the following accommodations: *preferential seating, provide individualized instruction when necessary, reduce/minimize distractions, stand near student when giving directions, calling him by name if necessary to assure that he's paying attention, break tasks and procedures into sequential steps when necessary, teach concrete concepts before teaching abstract concepts, modify/repeat/model directions, provide instruction in social skills and for standardized tests, administer to student in either secluded or smaller group setting (i.e., LEAP test for 2003-04 school year).*

Eric got his second round of braces before school was out and would wear them for two years. This time around, he didn't keep his hands in his mouth, and the experience wasn't as difficult or uncomfortable for him.

Eric made good grades his seventh-grade year and was recognized at the end-of-the-year awards program with a certificate for "A-B" honor roll. He also received the award for Outstanding Student in American History.

As soon as school was out, Eric went to Arkansas with Stinson and his family for a few days. The boys had a great time fishing in a pond on Stinson's grandparents' property. After the vacation, Eric started art lessons. In July, he went to Caney Camp in Minden, Louisiana, a church camp sponsored by the United Methodist Church, and later that month, our family went to Hot Springs, Arkansas, for a long weekend.

We saw Dr. Horton in June, and we told her we would like to try Eric on the 24-hour acting, non-stimulant drug Strattera. It would take two weeks for the drug to get into his system, so she had to keep Eric on the Metadate for a while longer. We had to watch Eric for continued ADHD symptoms as well as any tics he might have as we made the changes in his medication. As always before we left her office, Dr. Horton told me to call her if there were problems before the next appointment, which was scheduled for July 22, six weeks later.

At the July appointment, Eric had lost 3 ½ pounds in six weeks and weighed 89 ½. His appetite was not good and he stayed in a "blah" mood. "Eric eats only what he likes and if he doesn't like it, he goes without eating," I reported. "He's not even eating all of what he likes on his plate," I wrote in my notes. "Offer him milkshakes," Dr. Horton recommended. She also told me to discontinue giving him the Metadate. "Taken with Prozac, the Strattera may cover his ADHD," Dr. Horton said. "If he's draggy, he no longer needs Metadate," she said. Strattera is specifically for ADHD, and it also might decrease his anxiety, she explained. We were fairly certain the medication was the cause of Eric's decreased appetite, and in taking Metadate and Strattera, Eric was hit hard because they both were known to cause decreased appetite as a side effect. Dr. Horton said she was pleased Eric was showing no signs of tics. I was to call her in a week to report on his progress.

I kept notes for the report to Dr. Horton, and I wrote, "extremely subdued, lacks emotion, concentration is off, hard to get conversation out of him, leveled out, seems worse since school started, having trouble keeping up with things, teachers have noticed a change, not talking, not motivated." His appetite still wasn't what it should be, either.

Even though Eric started his school year in a quiet, subdued manner, unlike the Eric of the past, his eighth-grade year was one of his best so far. He was maturing, growing and studying hard, making "A's" and "B's" on his report card in his seven classes of Louisiana history, reading, language arts, math, science, enrichment and P.E.

I had talked with two of Eric's teachers before the next Dr. Horton appointment. On September 8, I met with Carmen Heflin, Eric's Louisiana history teacher, who reported he was not doing his work in class. Mrs. Heflin said the only homework she gave was class work that wasn't finished. "He's waiting until he gets home (to do his homework). He's wanting me to help him with everything," I wrote in my notes. Mrs. Heflin said Eric is very quiet in class and "not talking to me at all like he did last year." Mrs. Van Hoose, Eric's reading and language arts teacher, reported

144

on September 12 that while Eric was not being the class clown this year, he's "very calm and needs his self-confidence built up."

The next day at his appointment with Dr. Horton, Eric told her he was happy, and his OCD wasn't getting in the way of his activities. He said he has "one good friend and one sort of girlfriend." He confided he didn't like to talk to his parents as much as he did in the past. Dr. Horton noted his eye blinking was less noticeable. I told Dr. Horton that Rob and I were trying to get Eric to be more independent and to build his self-esteem level. She recommended Eric see psychologist Dr. Hill again to help Eric build his self-confidence and to help him with his organizational skills.

Our family took a weekend trip in October to Memphis, Tennessee, for the sole purpose of visiting Graceland, home of Elvis Presley, Kurt's favorite singer/performer. We thought it would be good therapy for everyone to get away for the weekend. While not being a big Elvis fan like his brother, Eric didn't seem to mind touring Elvis' home, trophy room and the Lisa Marie airplane and seeing the various array of automobiles and motorcycles once owned by the King of Rock and Roll. We spent several hours at Graceland but also visited Sun Studios, where Elvis recorded a handful of his early records, and we rode the Mud Island monorail that connects downtown Memphis to Mud Island River Park. Probably the most fun Eric had, though, was taking a running start and trying to see how far he could scale the side of the Great American Pyramid, a 32-story steel and glass replica of an Egyptian pyramid, located near the banks of the Mississippi River. He and Kurt spent several minutes showing off their Spiderman techniques.

In November, we saw Dr. Horton and reported Eric was doing very well on his medication of Prozac and Strattera and was on an even keel all day. He was not as hyperactive, he was sleeping and eating well, and he had "an excellent report from school." Eric told Dr. Horton he was mostly happy, had no OCD symptoms, was able to concentrate and was making good grades.

The only concern Eric had was a bullying situation at school. Bobby and a couple of the other boys in Eric's gym class had begun taunting him and twice came up behind him and pulled down his P.E. shorts, and his underwear came down with them. Fortunately only the boys in the gym class were around, but it both embarrassed and angered Eric.

After our Memphis trip, Eric started on a project for his reading/language arts class. The project was to create a Christmas notebook that had several activities, a few of which were writing assignments. One such assignment was a letter to the Grinch to convince him not to steal Christmas. Eric's letter, dated November 15, 2003, follows:

November 15, 2003

Dear Mr. Sorry Grinch,

I'm just writing you to convince you not to steal Christmas. You see, Christmas is a very special holiday that everyone enjoys. If you stole Christmas, all the kids would be unhappy, and eventually you would be unhappy to see the looks on all the kids' faces. Even you, Mr. Grinch, should enjoy Christmas; it is the most popular celebration of the year.

Christmas is the time when we celebrate the birth of Jesus, who is the Son of God. Jesus was born in Bethlehem a very long time ago. There were some wise men who brought special gifts to the baby Jesus, and this tradition of giving gifts has been passed down to all of us.

God has blessed this holiday, and wants us to remember it. I know you wouldn't want to disappoint God, so my advice to you is to leave Christmas alone and don't steal it from anyone. So think about it, and you will see what I mean.

Sincerely,

Eric A. Vardeman

Another assignment for the Christmas notebook was to interview someone about her Christmas memory and write about it.

Eric chose his grandmother—Rob's mom—and she gave him information for this story:

My grandma's Christmases when she was a little girl were different from mine today. Her family's Christmas trees were live trees cut down in the woods and were unlike the artificial tree my family has. The decorations that they put on the tree were gumballs covered in aluminum foil, pine burrs sprayed with gold paint and popcorn and paper chains. We have colored lights, fancy ornaments, sparkling garland and a large angel on top of our tree.

She and her brothers and sisters got very few presents back then because they didn't have as much money as we do today. I usually get at least some of the things on my Christmas list. They got gifts, fireworks, fruit and candy. I get a lot of gifts such as a bicycle, computer games, sports equipment and music.

They would eat a typical Christmas dinner on Christmas Eve, and sometimes sing Christmas carols in the neighborhood. On Christmas Eve, my family and I eat a Christmas meal at my grandparents' house, and we go to a Christmas Eve Holy Communion service at church. On Christmas Day, we eat lunch at my aunt's house.

Even though we celebrate Christmas differently than my grandma did, we still spend time with family, and the meaning of Christmas is still the same and will always be. The meaning is celebrating the birth of Jesus.

For "My Most Memorable Christmas," Eric chose to incorporate some fiction into his story:

My most memorable Christmas was when I went to Marshall, Texas, to see the Christmas lights. My whole family went—my mom and my dad, my brother Kurt and I. It was really cool.

There were Christmas lights all over the place, red and green flashing lights. There was frozen concrete where people could ice skate. There was a lot of stuff to do. Then we left to go home.

While riding in the car on the way home, I saw Santa's sleigh up in the sky. I told my dad to stop the car so my brother and I could see Santa. We stopped and got out where Santa's sleigh had landed. Kurt and I got out of the car to see him. We told Santa what we wanted for Christmas and he jotted it down on a piece of paper.

I said goodbye and we drove off. That night as I was about ready to go to bed, I wondered if that was the real Santa. On Christmas day as I opened my presents I was amazed, because I had gotten exactly what I had asked for. This is the story of my most memorable Christmas.

In February 2004, we saw Dr. Horton and reported Eric's grades were very good with four "A's" and three "B's." He was preparing to take the 8th-grade LEAP test in March, and he wasn't exhibiting any OCD symptoms. He was doing well at home, at school and socially, I told her.

Also that month, we had Eric's IAP. Accommodations listed were exactly the same as the ones listed on his 7th-grade IAP. I was grateful Eric was able to take the LEAP test in a secluded classroom with no distractions. He passed all areas of the test, and we were elated. His score in English Language Arts was higher than the state average. He scored 100% on the Use Conventions of Language section, but I also was pleased with his seven-out-of-12 score on Read, Analyze, and Respond to Literature and his 14-out-of-18 score on Apply Reasoning and Problem-Solving Skills. These scores showed marked improvement in Eric's reading comprehension. His math score was only four points below the state average, and his best score in the math section was 8.5 out of 13 in Measurement. He scored lowest in Algebra, answering only two out of nine questions correctly.

We reported the good news of Eric's LEAP results to Dr. Horton on May 11. Eric's mood was good and things were going well with the exception of the occasional problem of being bullied at school and an excessive focus on video games.

One of the programs near the end of the year was a talent show, and Eric participated by showing off his skill of walking on his hands across the gymnasium stage to the song 'Wipeout" by the Safaris. We remembered back when he was a small child and worked and worked on walking on his hands on our living room floor. He became so good at it, that the school cheerleaders would often ask him to do it for them.

At the May 13 end-of-school awards program, Eric was honored for his grades and received another award in the field of history, this time as Outstanding Student in *World* History. His grades had been good his eighth-grade year with all "A's" and "B's," and he made all "A's" the fourth nine weeks of school. We were extremely pleased with Eric's progress and showered him with praise.

Chapter Eighteen

Ready for High School

During the spring, Rob and I had been researching local high schools to determine where Eric would attend ninth through 12th grades. Although we liked UCP, there were some financial problems, and several teachers had resigned. We didn't want to start Eric in high school and then have to move him, so we decided to let him start ninth grade in the school from which he would graduate. We decided to enroll him at Calvary Baptist Academy, the same school where Stinson's parents had decided to send him. Several other UCP students and teachers were going to transfer there, also.

To get into Calvary, Eric had to take a test, and he didn't pass it. I met with Rhonda Honea, Calvary's principal, and explained Eric's disabilities and that he had qualified for accommodations under Section 504. She agreed to let him retake the test. He answered more questions correctly the second time, but he didn't finish the test. Calvary did not receive federal aid for students with disabilities, and the school would not allow Eric extended time on the exam. As a result, Mrs. Honea did not know whether to accept Eric as a student. I called Martha Maple from The Reading Center, and she wrote a letter to the Calvary administration asking that Eric be accepted into the school. The school made the decision to allow Eric to be admitted based on Mrs. Maple's letter and our agreeing to put Eric back into tutoring at The Reading Center.

We had bought Eric a suit and tie for his eighth grade graduation that he also wore on Easter Sunday in April. A few days earlier, my 88-year-old mother, who had colon cancer as well as rheumatoid and osteoarthritis, had decided to go into a nursing care facility. After church, still dressed in our Sunday Easter clothes, we visited her. She remarked about how handsome Eric looked in his suit and talked to him about his upcoming eighth-grade graduation. A little more than a month later, she died after having undergone emergency surgery. It was hard to lose her. She and Eric had a close relationship, and she had been supportive in all areas of Eric's life and particularly concerned with the struggles he faced. Eric was brokenhearted. He wore his new suit to her funeral on May 24, and later that evening, he graduated from eighth grade as one of the class' seven honor students.

The graduation was at University Worship Center in Shreveport and featured a slide presentation of the class' 13 graduates. We had been asked to submit five photos of Eric, from birth to present, and I enjoyed going through my many volumes of photos of him and choosing five that represented his life. I cried throughout the graduation, particularly when the pictures of Eric were shown on the screen in the worship center. I was so proud of him and his accomplishments, and I knew both my parents would have been proud of him, too.

Eric enjoyed a wonderful opportunity during the summer, participating in Weekend of the Cross through our church. Weekend of the Cross is a Thursday- through-Sunday program sponsored by the United Methodist Church and allows youth—with adult workers as supervisors—to work in the community, much like Habitat for Humanity. Participants stay at Centenary College in Shreveport, go out into the community to work, and have worship services and group meetings in the evenings. With that experience, Eric discovered within himself a desire to help others. He was so proud of the work he and his group did, he wanted to drive by the house he worked on and let us see the wheelchair ramp he helped build. A week or so later, our youth director, Tony Nations, asked Eric to speak in church about his experience, and Eric talked excitedly about building the ramp and how they had to build a turn in it to reach the house's front door. He spoke without any notes, and I was beaming at him from my seat in the choir loft.

Eric started ninth grade at Calvary Baptist Academy on August 16, 2004, with an orientation day. The campus, located at Calvary Baptist Church, was a lot larger than the ones at his previous schools, and I was glad to see that one of the handouts was a map.

Rob took Eric to his Dr. Horton appointment the next day, and she noted some "very mild facial tics." One other thing that was noticeable was Eric's weight gain. Although still slim, Eric had gained some weight within the past year from 94 pounds in September 2003, to 102 ¼ in February 2004, to 108 ¼ in May 2004 to 115 ½ in August 2004. He also had grown in height from 62 ¼" to 65 ¼." Either the Ritalin he had taken for years was keeping his weight off, he was growing very rapidly or both.

As soon as I could arrange meetings, Rob and I met with all of Eric's teachers except one—Jennifer Pixley, his art teacher—because he had her as a teacher at UCP. The teachers were willing to do what they could for Eric even though Calvary did not provide accommodations. At least he could be seated near the front of the class. In addition to art, Eric was enrolled in Algebra 1, English 1, world geography, physical science, P.E./health and Bible.

Eric continued to receive homework support from Rob and me, and I continued to make study guides for tests. Eric did well in Bible and art in particular. At tutoring, Mr. Maple helped Eric with science and other subjects while focusing on reading comprehension.

Rob and I had an opportunity to go to Hawaii in late September with my sister, brother-in-law and our close family friend, Glenda Humphreys, whose daughter lives on the island of Maui. We spent about 10 days on Maui and Oahu islands and left the boys in good hands back home with Rob's parents. After we returned, we were somewhat surprised to find that Eric had refused his grandmother's help with his homework, saying he could do it himself. From that time forward, Eric took charge of his own work, only occasionally asking me for help with English and his dad for help with math. *Maybe we should have gone to Hawaii a few years sooner*, we thought. This was a big step for Eric, and we continued to praise him for taking on the responsibility.

Rob took Eric to his appointment in November with Dr. Horton, and he reported Eric had made all "A's" and "B's" on his report card the second nine weeks of school and was on the honor roll. He also told her we had suspended tutoring because Eric was doing so well with his grades and he was working independently on his homework. In addition, he also was sleeping well, eating well and had "normal" energy. Dr. Horton said at Eric's next visit, which would be prior to the school year's end, we would discuss plans for any decreases of medication during the summer.

At the next appointment in February, we discussed decreasing Eric's Prozac after the school year ended. We would have to watch closely for anxiety or OCD symptoms, though, remembering the difficulty Eric went through when he was in the first grade and had depression and anxiety problems. Dr. Horton noticed Eric was blinking his eyes hard and asked him about it. He told her he didn't notice he was blinking his eyes but sometimes other people noticed he was blinking. He told her he was making new friends, getting along well with others and was happy.

Eric was doing well in his art class, making several grades in the upper 90 percentile. I was so impressed with one of his pieces, I had it framed and hung it on the wall in his room. I'm certain the school art class and art lessons during the summers at the Barnwell Center helped, but Eric had a gift for art.

In March, he received a letter from the school that said his grade-point average of 3.0 or above had identified him as a potential candidate for the Calvary Baptist Academy Chapter of the National Junior Honor Society (NJHS). He had met the criteria for GPA but also would be evaluated for the other four qualities of leadership, service, citizenship and character. He had to complete an information form and return it to the school by the April 5 deadline. With Eric's participation in Weekend of the Cross and other service projects through the youth group at our church, he had a lot of prior community service items to include. I was so happy for him. Of all of the good things that had happened to Eric thus far in his life, in my opinion, this was the best of all. If accepted, Eric would be recognized for his hard-earned grades.

We left on March 28 for a Spring Break vacation to Washington, D.C., with a side trip to New York City. We traveled with some other relatives and friends, nine of us making the trip and finding the weather, especially in New York, to be quite cold. We took an evening tour of the monuments, visited the Smithsonian, Arlington National Cemetery, National Archives Building, Mount Vernon, Virginia, U.S. Senator Jim McCrery's (R-La) office and had our photo made in front of the White House. Eric bought a Paul Revere-style hat, and he wore it constantly during the trip and on many occasions after we returned home. His favorite museum of the Smithsonian was the Museum of Natural History, where he spent a lot of time looking at the animal replicas. On our day trip to New York, we went to the top of the Empire State Building, visited Ground Zero and took a bus tour of the city.

About a week after we returned home, Eric received a letter dated April 12, 2005, from Calvary Baptist Academy. The first paragraph contained one word—*Congratulations!!* Eric had been accepted into the NJHS. The induction ceremony with a reception following was scheduled for April 26. Rob, his mom and I attended the ceremony, and in all my excitement of the evening and making sure I had my camera, I didn't remember to have Eric wear a tie, so he had to borrow one from another student who was already a member. As is the custom of being inducted into the honor society, Eric lit a candle, and he was handed his certificate by Mrs. Honea, the Calvary principal. His friend Stinson also was inducted, and I took several photos of the two friends during the evening. I felt we'd all been blessed beyond measure.

Chapter Nineteen

Bad Thoughts Getting in the Way

With all of these good things happening in Eric's life, we finally could breathe a sigh of relief and say a prayer of thanks that Eric was doing so well. He had overcome many obstacles, and his future was looking bright. But just when we were able to relax a little, Eric began to have another problem that was very worrisome to both him and us. He began to have some negative thoughts about God, which he expressed to us. These thoughts were something Eric had to battle and were very upsetting to him. He always had been a spiritual child and young man, and he was hurting inside because of these thoughts. At our April visit with Dr. Horton, he discussed with her thoughts about "not liking God very much and about violence." He said the thoughts "started earlier this year then went away and now have come back." He said about God, "I think I love him, but now I'm not sure." Dr. Horton and Eric spent some time discussing OCD again—that involuntary thoughts were like hiccups and he wasn't responsible for them.

The next month we went back to see Dr. Horton, and Eric reported the same thing had happened again. He told her the bad thoughts about God got better, went away, then came back the past week or two, but they were "not as much as before." He revealed feeling "mostly happy," but if he was quiet and not doing anything, the thoughts came back and worried him. Although Dr. Horton noted Eric was "guarded" and it was difficult for him to describe his experience, Eric disclosed another concern: Sometimes he felt grownups could hear his thoughts out loud. He said he felt people knew he had done something wrong or knew he was having bad thoughts. He told the psychiatrist he realized other people could not hear his thoughts out loud, but this was something that was going through his mind.

After discussing the risks and benefits with us, Dr. Horton prescribed Risperdal, a drug used to treat bi-polar disorder in adults and to treat anxiety associated with autism in children and youth. Although Eric didn't take the drug but a few times, it seemed to help the anxiety symptoms. Dr. Horton also urged us to take Eric to see Laurie Nussbaum, the licensed clinical social worker whom she had recommended four years earlier. Eric's OCD symptoms were severe at the time and were getting in the way of how he was handling things socially. We badly wanted to get some help for him. Eric had his first visit with Mrs. Nussbaum on May 28 shortly after school was out for the summer. With Eric's diagnoses of Asperger's and OCD, Mrs. Nussbaum's initial treatment goal in individual sessions was to focus primarily on techniques to use for managing the symptoms.

"The OCD symptoms (are) interfering with his social skills," Mrs. Nussbaum noted. A lack of social skills is one of the primary characteristics of Asperger's. The social worker said Eric was a "real trouper" in having to deal with a "double whammy" in having OCD along with Asperger's. "It is difficult enough just to learn how to deal with social skills," she said.

She taught Eric some techniques to help manage his OCD symptoms. One technique was a mental imagery exercise involving Eric's pretending to be in his favorite place, which Eric chose as Little Missouri Falls near Albert Pike, Arkansas. Tucked deep in the Arkansas woods, Little Missouri Falls, an offshoot of the Little Missouri River, is made up of an upper and lower falls. At the lower falls, the water tumbles over large rocks at it makes its way down to natural swimming holes. As a part of the exercise, Eric wrote all the details he could recall for each sense—what he saw, heard, smelled, etc. When he became anxious or experienced bad OCD thoughts, he immediately would take a pretend trip to Little Missouri Falls in his mind. As Mrs. Nussbaum explains, the relaxation technique is widely used to stop bad thoughts and allow the person to replace them with positive, happy, relaxed thoughts.

Another technique Mrs. Nussbaum taught Eric to use was a "Comfort Sheet" to stop negative thoughts and replace them with positive thoughts. Eric and Mrs. Nussbaum created a personal

"Comfort Sheet" that targeted his negative OCD thoughts with certain responses. "The idea behind this is that if you can stop the thought before it is a complete sentence in your mind, you can stop the anxiety," she explained. "The anxiety is what causes us to act (compulsion). The act could be more thoughts or actual physical acts."

Both techniques—the mental imagery exercise and the Comfort Sheet—can be used for anxiety in social settings, Mrs. Nussbaum said.

Eric attended five individual therapy sessions and a handful of group sessions, the latter targeting social skills and focusing on discussing and role-playing. Topics covered were "Starting a Conversation," "Being Aware of Body Language—Learning What Certain Social Cues Mean," "Eye Contact," "Reflective Listening," "How To Be Assertive," "How to Deal with Bullies," "How to Learn to Stay in Control," "Keep Your Power," "How to Not Worry About What Others Think" and "Realizing That We Cannot Control Others' Feelings."

When the individuals were not working on role-playing, they were playing board and card games as they discussed issues. "Playing games with other children in a group setting is a wonderful tool in itself," Mrs. Nussbaum said.

Eric gained valuable tools from his individual and group visits with Laurie Nussbaum, just as he had with Dr. Hill and Dr. Horton. I very much appreciate their work with Eric and realize his life would be very different if it had not been for them. I was glad he didn't have to continue taking Risperdal or any other anti-anxiety drug to combat the negative thoughts.

The summer after his freshman year was a busy time for Eric. On June 11, he took the American College Testing (ACT) so he could have practice before his senior year when the test score needed to be as high as possible. In Louisiana, students can qualify for a Taylor Opportunity Program for Students (TOPS) scholarship if they score a minimum composite 20 on the ACT. With his 504 qualifications and a letter from Dr. Horton regarding his diagnosis of Asperger's Syndrome, Eric was able to have extended time on the test. He scored a 15 on his first attempt (top score is 36), which I thought was a good first score for him.

He saw Dr. Horton on June 22 and told her at times he was better able to control the bad thoughts than others. He was working that summer at Disc Daddy, the music store Rob owns that sells new and used compact discs, movies and games. The work helped him stay active and keep his mind occupied on other things.

Church camp at Caney Lake in Minden was where Eric spent part of five days in June. Also that month, he took driver's education at a local driving school that included classroom instruction and driving with an instructor and received his learner's permit. His instructor wrote the following comments about Eric's driving time with him:

Enjoyed driving with Eric. He did a great job. He is on his way to becoming a safe driver.

In July, Eric participated again in Weekend of the Cross and had another good experience with other young people and serving others in the community who are less fortunate. A trip to Hot Springs, Arkansas, in August rounded out the summer for us.

By the time Eric saw Dr. Horton in early August, the bad thoughts he was having had dissipated to only about one per week and they were not lingering. We had left off the Risperdal, and he was doing fine without it. He told Dr. Horton he was happier and ready to be a 10th-grader.

Chapter Twenty

A Move to the City and Busy School Days

Eric's sophomore year proved to be another academically successful year for him in high school, although he had some difficulty in Spanish I. For some reason, he had a hard time learning a second language. The first two nine weeks, he made "C's" in the class but then brought the grades up to "B's" the third and fourth nine weeks. In addition to Spanish, he had English II, civics/free enterprise, Bible, biology, geometry and P.E.

On September 30, we moved from the Blanchard area to the Broadmoor Terrace subdivision in Shreveport so we could be closer to our jobs and the schools where Eric and Kurt attended. I had gone back to work full-time in the oil and gas industry at St. Mary Land & Exploration Company (now SM Energy Company) in June 2004, and Rob's Disc Daddy store was in Shreve City, a shopping center near our new home. At first, the boys missed the nearby woods of our previous neighborhood, but soon they were happy about not having to be in the car so much. Once Eric got his driver's license in March 2006, he was able to drive himself to tennis lessons and to school during his junior and senior years.

Throughout his school years, Rob and I encouraged Eric to do extra credit for his classes. One of the projects in his sophomore English class was to do a report on a potential career. It was one of the best assignments he had that year because for the first time, Eric did some serious thinking about what career he might like to pursue. Having loved animals all his life, Eric reported on wildlife management, and he interviewed people who worked for nature parks and the state forestry service.

In November, Eric told Dr. Horton he had been bored after school was out in the afternoons and had started tennis lessons. This was the first time he had been involved in sports since he took gymnastics when he was much younger. He loved tennis and practiced at a local high school on afternoons when he wasn't taking lessons. Eric reported to Dr. Horton school was going well, he was making good grades, his appetite and sleep were good as was his energy level. He had occasional OCD thoughts, he said, "but I can control them," and they weren't getting in the way of life's activities.

Before the end of the calendar year, Eric took the Preliminary SAT/National Merit Scholarship Qualifying Test. He was not allowed extended time, and his test results reflected that. He scored highest in Writing Skills with a 42 (higher than 44% of sophomores), a 33 in Math (higher than 13% of sophomores) and a 20 in Critical Reading (higher than 1% of sophomores).

We visited Dr. Horton in February, and Eric told her he was mostly happy and there were no OCD symptoms getting in his way. I reported Eric was spending a lot of time in his room. He was maturing both emotionally and physically and had grown to 5'7'' and weighed 145 ¼ pounds. He was staying busy with schoolwork, tennis and working for his dad at Disc Daddy. Eric was very good at remembering what CDs and movies had been bought and were in the store and easily helped customers find appropriate movies for their children. He quickly could tell them every movie Johnny Depp or most any other popular actor was in and if the store carried the title at the time. This was quite an accomplishment because at times, Rob's store might have as many as 3,000 movies in various categories. Just as he memorized music facts when he was young, Eric learned what year CDs and movies were released. With movies, he could name the actors in them, knew what they were rated and give facts about the plot.

Eric took the Iowa Test in the spring, scoring high in spelling, grammar and sentence structure, scoring average in math and low in science and social studies. Analyzing data and using critical thinking skills were still problems for Eric, as the standardized test results showed.

Also in the spring, a letter came from Eric's school announcing that he met the required GPA (3.4 or higher) for selection into the National Honor Society. He had to have a

160

minimum of 30 hours of service from January 2005 to March 2006. We completed the information form with Eric's activities listed, and Eric was accepted. The induction ceremony was held on May 11, 2006, and this time I remembered his tie. The inductees were given a certificate and a yellow rose after they walked across the stage and lit their candles. My sister, brother-in-law, Rob and I attended the ceremony in the Calvary Worship Center.

A couple of weeks before the NHS ceremony, on April 30, my best friend, Glenda Humphreys, died of ovarian cancer after a four-year, four-month-long battle with the disease. She was a tower of strength even when she was weak from chemotherapy, and her positive attitude was amazing. Glenda had said many prayers for Eric throughout his life for the difficulties he faced. I'm sure she prayed for Rob and me, too, as we dealt with Eric's Asperger's Syndrome. I am thankful to God that she was a part of our lives for the years we knew her and her family. Her husband, Charles, was the pastor that led Eric's confirmation class. He had died suddenly of a heart condition in September 2003.

Eric took his driver's test on May 3 and didn't pass it because he didn't come to a complete stop at a stop sign. On his second attempt, he passed and got his driver's license. Even though he was "official," we were selective on when we let him drive alone.

There were no OCD problems or concerns to report to Dr. Horton on May 15. She noted that his mood was good, and he told her he had good grades and he was looking forward to the end of school.

The youth choir at our church had an opportunity to join the youth choir at First United Methodist Church of Shreveport on a chartered bus choir tour out West. Eric and Kurt both went as part of the youth choir, and I went as a chaperone. Of the many places we visited and things we did, Eric was the most thrilled at the animals he encountered at the Grand Canyon's North Rim. He took a great photo of a deer trotting through the campground, and he was completely at ease on the back of the mule he rode on a trail down into the canyon.

We returned from the trip in time for Eric to take the ACT in June. This time, he scored a 17, two points higher than he did the previous year.

In July, Eric underwent nasal surgery for a deviated septum. He had been suffering with nosebleeds for several months and had to have his nose cauterized a couple of months prior to the surgery. He had suffered for years with allergy problems, and the surgery and regular allergy shots helped alleviate the majority of the problems.

When Eric saw Dr. Horton later that month, he revealed that he sometimes felt bored at his new house in the city when he wasn't playing tennis, visiting with Stinson or working at Rob's store. He'd had a busy summer with the trip out West and with our family vacation to Gulf Shores, but he told Dr. Horton that he was ready for school to start. He said he wasn't having any obsessive-compulsive thoughts that he couldn't control.

Eric's next-to-last year of high school began in August with the following class schedule: American history, Spanish II, fine arts survey, English III, chemistry, Algebra II and Bible.

In September, Eric brought home a brochure and information for ordering his senior ring. I helped him pick it out, but when he ordered it, he came home and told me it didn't cost as much as we thought it would. "I saved you some money," he told me and showed me his selection of a cheaper, yet nice-looking, ring. I asked him if his selection was the one he really wanted, and he said it was. That was my concern—that he was happy with the ring. It was white gold with a green stone (one of Calvary's school colors and Eric's favorite color) and had "Cavs" (short for Cavaliers, the school mascot) on one side and "2008" and a tennis racquet on the other.

The two previous years Eric was at Calvary, I had encouraged him to go to the Homecoming dance. He had no interest in it, however, until he was a junior. That year he asked a couple of girls to go, but they were all going as a group, so he went without a date, as did his friend Stinson, and had a great time.

Stinson was in the Beta Club, an educational organization for high school students whose qualifications are good character, scholastic achievement and a commendable attitude. He talked to Eric about applying for membership. Eric applied and was selected, just in time to participate in the District Beta Rally on October 31 in Minden.

When Eric saw Dr. Horton in October, he told her he was having some OCD symptoms but they were not causing him problems. Worrying about what other people thought of him was a problem he discussed with her. Otherwise he reported he was happy and he was doing fine socially.

Eric took the PSAT/NMSQT again before the year's end, and with this standardized test, his Mathematics score, at 37, was his highest of the three testing areas. Next was Writing Skills at 36 and then Critical Reading at 30. As was the case the previous year, Eric did not have extended time to take the test. It would have been interesting to see if there was much of a difference in test scores if Eric had been allowed extended time.

The junior class would be taking a trip to Washington, D.C., in the spring, and Eric was excited to be going back to the nation's capital, this time with his classmates instead of his family. There were several meetings to attend to prepare for the trip, and Rob and I worked in the concession stand at the Cavalier football games to earn money toward Eric's trip.

The State Beta Club Convention was January 17-19 in Lafayette, and Eric participated in spelling. He didn't win, but I was happy for him to have had the experience.

There were no OCD symptoms to report to Dr. Horton at Eric's appointment in January. With Eric's now driving alone to school and tennis lessons, we kept a close watch on him to make sure he was not having any OCD or ADHD symptoms that might interfere with his operating a vehicle.

The spring was packed with trips and activities, and Eric was enjoying every minute of his junior year. The NHS took a day field trip to the Louisiana Baptist Children's Home in Monroe to tour the facilities.

Earlier that spring, we had gotten Eric a cell phone because we were letting him drive to school. We were not aware until the bill arrived Eric was using it to access the Internet. He ran up charges of $50.00 the second or third month he had the phone and didn't argue when we told him he would have to pay us back for it. He didn't have a job at the time other than working for Rob, but he reimbursed us each week until he repaid his debt.

The junior class' Washington trip was March 21-23, and although it was only part of three days, the class packed in more in those days than we did in 2005. They visited Arlington National Cemetery, toured the monuments and memorials, stopped by the White House and toured Ford's Theater and the Peterson House, the National Archives, Holocaust Museum, Mount Vernon, the Capitol, the Natural History Museum and the Air and Space Museum.

During Spring Break week, our family and a family friend went to Las Cruces and Carlsbad Caverns, New Mexico. Eric spent a lot of time catching lizards and checking out the desert wildlife.

That spring Eric attended some ACT prep classes on Saturdays to better prepare him for the April 14 ACT test. He scored a 19 on this third attempt. Thus far, he had increased his score by two points each time he took the test. He was very close to the score of 20 he needed to qualify for the TOPS scholarship for college.

Although Eric had been participating in the Beta Club since the fall, he wasn't formally recognized as a member until the induction ceremony on April 12, when he received his certificate and pin.

So far this was the best April Eric ever had. It was so much better than many past Aprils when, as a child, he was afraid of

164

thunder and bad weather or suffered from anxiety issues.

Chapter Twenty-One

The Prom, A Senior Ring and A Job

Eric asked one of his classmates, Amanda Lee, to the junior-senior prom. She accepted, and we spent a Friday evening in a formal wear store for Eric to be fitted for his tux. He was a handsome young man in his black tux with a red tie that matched Amanda's red dress. We met Amanda, another couple and their parents at the Calvary campus before the prom to take photos. We were relieved Amanda's mom had offered to drive the two couples to the dinner and the dance in her van so that none of the students had to drive.

Eric had been filling out employment applications for a few weeks, and was hired to work as a stocker at Drug Emporium, a discount drug store, located a few blocks from our home. He was scheduled to begin work on Tuesday, April 15. About 7 a.m. on April 14, Eric was driving our 1994 Toyota Camry to a gym to work out. He was a few minutes behind Rob, who was also going to work out. Unfortunately, Eric made a left turn in front of a car that was partially blocked in his view by another vehicle. The cars collided, and Eric's car was hit on the passenger side. Both air bags in the Camry deployed, and Eric received a few cuts and a sprained finger. The woman driving the other car was shaken up but not injured. Thankfully, Eric was not given a citation due to some other factors involving the accident but was understandably upset. When I arrived on the scene, I hugged him and reassured him that everything was going to be fine. Rob and I took him to the emergency room, and he was treated for his cuts and sprain. After the accident, Eric became a more careful, cautious driver. The Camry was totaled, and we bought a 1998 Toyota Corolla for Eric to drive.

One of the best things for Eric was starting to work at Drug Emporium the day after his wreck because it got his mind off the accident. After school was out for the day, he reported for work.

166

Following his five-hour shift, he came home, and with great detail, told us about his first day on the job and showed us his store-issued box cutter knife. He was given a schedule I kept on my calendar for the first couple of weeks. After that, he diligently kept up with his own hours and always reported to work on time. He worked at Drug Emporium through his junior and senior year and continues his employment there as I write this today.

We visited Dr. Horton on April 28, and the only concern I had was Eric was sleeping a lot and seemed to be listless. He was sleeping so much sometimes he missed tennis lessons, and we would have to wake him up if we needed to go somewhere in the evenings. He told Dr. Horton he was "mentally tired of school and physically tired." He had complained to us of being bored and tired of school, but he didn't seem depressed and had a good appetite. Eric told Dr. Horton there were no OCD symptoms getting in the way, but he was just eager for school to be out. He was able to focus and study, but he said he was sleepy in class. She suggested after his finals were over, we should leave off the Strattera unless his symptoms were problematic.

On May 8, Eric received his senior ring in a ceremony at the school and was beginning to see the end of the prep school tunnel. A couple of months later, he had his senior pictures taken in his cap and gown and wearing khakis and a blue shirt that matched his eyes.

Later that month, I received a notice for placing an ad in Eric's senior yearbook. I already knew what I wanted the ad to look like, and as soon as I received the notice, I went to work on it. It was a half-page ad with green letters at the top reading, "Eric, we are proud of you." There were four photos, one of which would be his senior picture that would be taken in the summer, a photo from the NHS induction ceremony, a photo of Eric wearing his tux on prom night, and a photo of Eric and Stinson showing off their senior rings. It included my favorite Bible verse from Jeremiah 29, one that I believe describes God's plan for Eric's life, "For I know the plans I have for you," declares the Lord, "plans to prosper you and not to harm you, plans to give you hope and a future." Underneath the verse was "Go Seniors 2008."

At the end of Eric's junior year, he had maintained a 3.4 GPA and had amassed four "A's," three "B's" and a "C." He had taken the Iowa Test in the spring, and the results were much like those of previous tests. He scored high in spelling and language arts, and low scores were recorded in analyzing information and concepts and problem solving.

After school was out, Eric and I went on a tour to the Bahamas with our church's youth choir and the First Methodist Church of Shreveport's youth choir. Kurt didn't want to go that year, but Eric was excited about the trip and ready to do some snorkeling. He spent a lot of time on the beach at our hotel in Nassau, checking out the sea urchins and even captured one on a small shovel, showing his catch to our group on the beach. He also joined part of the group that went snorkeling and observed sharks that were later fed fish off the boat.

Eric saw Dr. Horton on June 30, and we talked about Eric's car wreck and his new job. I also told her we had left off the Strattera the week before we went to the Bahamas, and Eric was doing fine without the ADHD medication. She said he could continue to leave off the Strattera unless we saw symptoms of inattentiveness. On August 2, Eric had his wisdom teeth extracted and had to miss a couple of days of work. The oral surgeon had told us to give him soft foods when he woke up enough to be hungry, but when the anesthesia wore off, Eric wanted "real food." He was still groggy and was being very assertive with me in demanding what he wanted to eat. He said something like, "I'm Eric Vardeman, and I have friends who respect me." It was very funny, and even though he was not supposed to eat anything but soft foods, I gave in and watched him devour a plate of meat, vegetables and bread.

Chapter Twenty-Two

Senior '08, A High School Graduate

Eric started his senior year at Calvary on August 15, 2007. When he drove off to school that morning, I couldn't help but think how fast time seemed to have gone. Weren't my sister and I taking Eric to pre-school just a few short years ago? He had come so far and overcome so many obstacles. I blinked back tears as a wave of emotion hit me. This unusual little boy who had played with strings, moved his hand like a fan blade and memorized lists of songs had grown into a fine young man and was on his way to becoming a successful adult.

Eric needed only four and a half credits to graduate, and he took pre-calculus, English IV, physics, Bible and a semester of business computer. He did well in English, Bible and the computer class but had some difficulty in pre-calculus, ending with a "C" for the fourth nine weeks and a "D" for the semester grade. He made "B's" in physics the first semester and ended with a "C" the second semester.

One of Eric's favorite pieces of clothing from his senior year was his senior spirit shirt, a black t-shirt with yellow and white lettering on the front with the message: "Calvary Baptist Academy, Senior 2008; Freshmen Follow Us, Sophomores Respect Us, Juniors Want To Be Us." On the back, "Seniors 2008" was in large yellow letters with signatures of each senior class member in white.

The fall was busy for Eric with another attempt at the ACT in October to score at least a composite 20 (he scored an 18), a Beta Club District Rally in Minden and a College/Career Fair in Shreveport, the latter two in November. The college fair featured booths from various colleges and universities in the state and solidified Eric's decision to study wildlife management/animal science at Louisiana State University-Shreveport (LSU-S). This was something he had discussed with his dad and me, expressing the desire to live at home and study at LSU-S. The program at the local university was a two-year pre-degree, so he planned to complete the first two years there and transfer to Louisiana Tech University in Ruston, my alma mater, to complete his four-year degree.

Group tennis lessons and working took up a lot of Eric's time when he wasn't doing homework or studying for tests, so he didn't have much idle time, something that was a goal of ours in order to keep him focused and content. He wasn't taking anything for his ADHD after having stopped the Strattera in May and was doing well without it. The only medication he was taking was Prozac for OCD symptoms. He told Dr. Horton in October he was focusing fine without the Strattera and there were no OCD symptoms getting in the way. He told her he was working out through lifting weights and exercising and trying to cut down on fast foods. Work at Drug Emporium was going well, and he was making good grades.

In December, Eric took the ACT again. It took several weeks to receive the test results, and we signed him up to take it again in February 2008 in case he didn't make a 20. Eric needed to bring his math score up on the ACT and he was struggling in pre-calculus, so we scheduled some math tutoring with a high school math teacher. It would be the first week of January before the ACT results came by mail. I retrieved the envelope out of the mailbox, whispered a quick prayer and opened the test results. Composite score—20! I'm sure I was shaking when I picked up the phone and called Rob at his store. I told him the news and then he put Eric, who was working there at the time, on the phone. I told him the score, and he was thrilled. Eric had qualified for a TOPS scholarship! The rank on the test score showed approximately 58% of the students taking the test scored at or below Eric's score. He scored 21 in English, 17 in mathematics, 21 in reading and 19 in science. The composite 20 qualified Eric for a TOPS Opportunity Award, the lowest level of TOPS granted, but it didn't matter. It was a huge accomplishment for Eric.

He told Dr. Horton about his ACT score at his appointment in January. He also reported that his grades were good, his concentration was fine and there were no OCD symptoms getting in the way.

The State Beta Convention was January 23-25 in Baton Rouge, and this time, Eric participated in English academic testing. Again he didn't win, but he enjoyed the experience and spending time with his classmates.

Our family took a Spring Break vacation to California, visiting Rob's sister in Durham and his cousin in San Francisco, who took us on a tour of the San Francisco Conservatory of Music where she is the dean. We spent one morning in San Francisco taking a bicycle ride over the Golden Gate Bridge. We took the ride early while the fog was still thick and we were unable to see very far ahead of us. By the time we headed back over the bridge, the fog had lifted, and we had a beautiful view of the Pacific Ocean and Alcatraz Island. Many years before, I had toured Alcatraz, where Al Capone, George "Machine Gun" Kelly and the Bird Man of Alcatraz were imprisoned, and I wanted Rob and the boys to see it. After we purchased our tickets, Eric bought an Alcatraz skull cap that kept his ears warm on the chilly boat ride to the island and back.

The boys, who were impervious to the cold air, enjoyed riding the streetcar while standing on the exposed outside and holding onto the bar. Rob and I preferred the inside where it was a bit warmer.

In Durham, Rob's sister taught us to shoot her handmade bows and arrows, took us to the yo-yo factory in Chico, where the world's largest yo-yo is located and on a long nature hike on a beautiful Northern California trail. Eric spotted a non-poisonous snake and picked it up, letting it slither over his arm. I snapped a picture of him and the snake and then got out of the way.

After we got back home, I started planning Eric's graduation party. Our church had a Senior Recognition Sunday honoring Eric and one other student who were graduating from high school. I wrote the following information for the program, which was read by the youth director:

Eric will graduate May 16 from Calvary Baptist Academy in Shreveport. Eric is 18 and has attended Calvary all four years of high school. During his high school years, Eric has been on the honor roll and the merit roll, has been a member of the National Honor Society, the Spanish Club and the Calvary chapter of the National Beta Club. The Beta Club is an organization that recognizes academic achievement, promotes character, develops leadership skills, encourages service involvement and provides technological advantages to students. One benefit of being in the Beta Club is being able to travel and compete in Beta conventions. Eric traveled to Lafayette during his junior year to compete in the spelling academic testing section and to Baton Rouge during his senior year to compete in English academic testing. During his junior year, Eric traveled to Washington, D.C., with his classmates and toured the U.S. Capitol, the Smithsonian and several memorials. Eric has been active in playing tennis during high school and took lessons at The Indoors at Pierremont Oaks.

As a part of his membership in the National Honor Society, Eric had to log in several hours of community service each year. Even though it was a requirement for the honor society, Eric's life was enriched by being involved in community service, and he found he has a yearning desire to help others. He was able to serve God and his fellow man by participating in Weekend of the Cross sessions during the summer at Centenary. Eric also participated in several Paint Your Heart Out Saturdays in May. He spent several hours helping his mom's friend load furniture into a moving van. He participated with other Lakeview members in a VIM trip to Abbeville, Louisiana, to help rebuild the community after the 2005 hurricanes Katrina and Rita. Other hours were earned by picking up trash along the South Lakeshore Drive section that was adopted by the Lakeview Youth group.

Eric has enjoyed his middle school and high school years as an active member of the Lakeview Youth group, and for the past two years, he has been a part of the Youth Choir from our church that was invited to join the First United Methodist-Shreveport

Youth Choir on its summer tour to the Grand Canyon in 2006 and the Bahamas in 2007.

Eric enjoys spending his free time weight-lifting and working out at home and at the gym. He also enjoys jogging and walking, but you won't see him doing this without his trusty IPod, because he loves music. Other hobbies are spending time and working at Disc Daddy, his dad's music store; spending time with friends; watching movies; and observing animals, particularly reptiles, a hobby that he did not inherit from his mother.

Being employed at Drug Emporium as a stocker for a little more than a year has given Eric a taste of what the working world is like. Eric has been promoted recently in his job, received a raise and was put in charge of the grocery deliveries on Mondays. He loves working at Drug Emporium and plans to continue working while he goes to college. Eric has been accepted and will attend Louisiana State University in Shreveport in the fall. He has a TOPS scholarship and plans to study wildlife management or animal science. He is enrolled at Bossier Parish Community College this summer and will be taking an English class.

Eric is thankful that he has been able to grow up in this church among such a loving, nurturing group of Christians.

The two seniors were honored with a reception following the worship service, and were showered with money, cards and good wishes for the future.

Eric got his senior yearbook, and he had it signed by numerous classmates and teachers. Amid the good wishes from his fellow classmates, there were some references to Eric's sense of humor:

Eric! Thanks for always making me laugh.

Wow, these past years has been a blast. Thanx 4 making me smile so much,

Hey, Eric! You have made me laugh these past years!

There also were some surprise comments, at least to Rob and me:

Eric, Don't change! I don't care what anyone tells you. You are a great guy.

Eric!! Never let anyone change who you are. Keep being you no matter what. And keep God #1.

Eric, Wow, what do I say? You are so much fun. Never change. You are

amazing and always make me laugh.

The yearbook also contained a huge blessing to us when we read a quote from a fellow senior. The heading at the top of one of the pages asked, "Who is the classmate that has inspired you most?" The young man wrote, "Eric Vardeman inspires me the most because he doesn't let people put labels on him."

Eric's last day of school was May 8, and between that day and his graduation, eight days later, I prepared for his graduation party and went shopping with a friend for something new to wear for the occasion. Several relatives had called after receiving invitations saying they were going to be at the graduation and party, so it was a hectic week.

On the evening of graduation, I took some pictures of Eric and Kurt as they worked on tying their ties. Kurt managed to get his tied first and was trying to help Eric. Rob was working and would meet us at the school for graduation, so he wasn't available to help, and I certainly didn't know how to tie a man's tie. Eric couldn't seem to get his tie looking right, and he needed to leave to be at the school early. We ended up having Eric take his tie off, put it around Kurt's neck, and Kurt tied it, loosened it and gave it back to Eric. With his green cap and gown in place, he took the white NHS collar and put it on, then draped the yellow Beta Club stole around his neck for the final touch. I had enough time to snap a few photos before Eric said he needed to leave. After a hug from Kurt and me, he was on his way.

Commencement was at Calvary Baptist Church Worship Center in Shreveport, and we arrived early enough to save a row of seats for family and a close friend. By the time everyone arrived, there were more relatives than seats, and some of them had to sit in the balcony. The commencement program booklet featured color photos of the 70 students and listed honors and club membership of each student. Eric's had Merit Roll, Honor Roll, Principal's List, National Honor Society, Beta Club and Spanish Club. The senior class produced a video featuring interviews with the class of 2008. The seniors talked about favorite teachers and people who inspire them. Eric mentioned his English teacher, Amy Rickets, and thanked her for teaching him "a lot about English."

When Eric's name was called, he walked across the stage and received his diploma, shaking hands and hugging the Calvary administrators along the way. I

could not have been more proud. I thought about something Rob told me when Eric was young and we were so worried about him and his future. "I think God gave Eric to us so we could help him," Rob had said. He was right. We were able to help Eric, and I'm so thankful God gave us the opportunity. I would not have wanted it any other way.

Appendix

Dyslexia Report Test Results (Office of 504/Dyslexia, Caddo Parish Schools) – October/November 1998

Criterion Referenced Spelling Test (CRST) – 94%. This test determines whether a child understands basic spelling patterns, such as consonant, vowel, consonant blends and non-phonetic words. Eric spelled correctly 30 of the 33 words, missing "thick" (fick), "mush" (much) and "speed" (speep). He correctly wrote the dictated sentence: "Today is a warm day." All of Eric's writing samples except the alphabet were written in manuscript. The letters were "legible" although they were not "consistently formed." When asked to write the alphabet, Eric asked if he needed to write the letters in cursive. He was told he could choose between cursive or print, and he wrote most of the capital and lower case letters mostly correctly in cursive. He wrote the days and the week and the months of the year correctly except misspelling "February" ("Febuary").

Primary Reading Skills test for coding skills. Eric was asked to write the letter that spells the sound for each word, and scored the following:

Initial consonants – 100%

Final consonants – 100%

Consonant blends – 100%

Consonant digraphs – 80%

Long vowels – 80%

Short vowels – 90%

Syllables – 80%

Slosson Oral Reading Test-Revised (SORT-R). This test contains a list of words that students should be able to read at various grade levels. Eric scored at the beginning of the fourth grade.

Diagnostic Reading Scales (DRS). The exam contains grade-level passages which Eric read aloud and was then asked questions. He read a 3.5 grade-level passage, substituting three of the 162 words and self-correcting two other words.

However, on the comprehension part, his score was inadequate, correctly answering only four of the eight questions. The answers that were incorrect were related to the story but did not give correct information. On another 3.5 grade-level passage that was read to him, Eric's comprehension was very poor, correctly answering only one of the eight questions correctly.

Comprehensive Receptive and Expressive Vocabulary Test (CREVT), a standardized test measuring oral language. On the receptive subtest, Eric was to point to a picture that is related to a spoken word, and on the expressive subtest, he had to tell what a word means that was spoken to him. Eric scored in the 3rd percentile for receptive and 30th percentile for expressive, with a total of 7th percentile (poor range).

Iowa Test scores – 2nd grade:

Reading Total – 4th percentile	Math comp – 29th percentile
Language Total – 25th percentile	Math prob – 4th percentile
Listening – 31st percentile	Science – 4th percentile
Total battery – 8th percentile	Social studies – 9th percentile

Diagnostic Reading and Math Testing (The Reading Center of Shreveport) – August 1999

Slosson Intelligence Test-Revised (a short intelligence test used as an individual screening instrument for both children and adults) – Eric is functioning in the average range with a mental age of nine years, five months (9.5, the age at which he took the test), with a percentile rank of fifty-five (55) and a stanine of five (5).

Peabody Picture Vocabulary Test-Third Edition (an estimate of an individual's receptive or hearing vocabulary in Standard English as compared with a cross-section of people in the United States of the same age). Eric's results are as follows:

Standard Score – 91

Percentile Rank – 27

Stanine – 4

Age equivalent – eight years, four months (8.4)

Slosson Oral Reading Test-Revised (a graded list of words ranging in difficulty from primer to high school level). Eric scored at the fourth grade, ninth month level (4.9) with a percentile rank of fifty-five (55) and a stanine of five (5).

Classroom Reading Inventory (an informal reading inventory for elementary and middle school students which tells the examiner a student's appropriate instructional level in reading). The results are as follows:

Passage Level	Word Recognition	Comprehension
Preprimer	Independent Level	Frustration Level
Primer	Independent Level	Instructional Level
First Grade	Instructional Level	Independent Level
Second Grade	Independent Level	Frustration Level
Third Grade	Independent Level	Frustration Level

Fourth Grade   Instructional Level   Instructional Level

Development Test of Visual Motor Integration-4th Revision (consists of 24 geometric shapes that the student must copy with the results indicating the student's ability to integrate visual and motor skills at a specific age equivalent). Eric scored an age equivalent of eight years, nine months (8.9) with a percentile rank of forty-five (45).

The Gates-MacGinitie Reading Test (a measure of vocabulary knowledge and silent reading comprehension). Eric scored as follows:

Test	Stanine	Percentile	Grade Equivalent
Vocabulary	3	11	2.6
Comprehension	3	22	2.5
TOTAL	3	16	2.6

Informal Dyslexia Screening Activities – Various aspects of literary acquisition are estimated through these informal activities. Eric wrote his name, address and phone number in manuscript, substituting "s" for "n" in the street name "Acorn." In writing the capital and lower case letters of the alphabet, he wrote the capital letters in manuscript and the lower case in cursive. He correctly recited in sequence the letters of the alphabet, months of the year and days of the week.

An informal auditory processing test was made up of repeating three, four and five unrelated letter or numeral sequences. Eric was able to repeat four of six sequences, but when asked to repeat the same letter/numeral sequences in reverse order, he was able to repeat only three of the six correctly. He was asked to copy a 29-word paragraph in manuscript and in correct order. The report said his handwriting was easy to read and with good proportion, spacing and rhythm.

In the spelling of 16 nonsense and English words, Eric spelled 10 correctly. Errors in spelling were one omission and five substitutions.

The Elementary Reading Attitude Survey (estimates a student's attitude toward recreational and academic reading). Eric exhibited a positive attitude toward both types of reading but said he did not like to do workbook pages and worksheets.

Percentile ranks: Recreational Reading: 66th percentile

                      Academic Reading   64th percentile

                      Full Scale   66th percentile

Behavioral observations – Eric entered the testing situation willingly, was friendly, talkative and "appeared to carefully, but readily, answer all questions throughout the evaluation." He was cooperative and seemed to put forth his best effort on each test section. He said that he read some but was not an avid reader, enjoying reading about snakes. Eric also said he liked to play basketball. He said the hardest thing about school was when he got things wrong. Before the end of the testing, Eric was exhibiting some anxiety about when he would be finished and if his mother had returned yet to pick him up.

Analysis and Recommendations – On the orally administered verbal intelligence screening, Eric's score was in the average range with a percentile rank of fifty-five (55). Mental age equivalent was nine years, five months (9.5) which measures at his chronological age and indicates that he has the mental capacity to handle academic material at his grade level with adequate instruction and support, "barring any unforeseen learning disability. " Eric's strongest area was in comprehension of everyday events. He had some difficulty with questions regarding short-term auditory memory and similarities/differences.

Eric's score on the receptive (hearing) vocabulary screening fell in the average range with a percentile rank of twenty-seven (27). His age equivalent score measured eight years, four months (8.4), below his chronological age. "This indicates that Eric would benefit from study to improve his vocabulary understanding." The test result report said that developing Eric's pleasure reading, playing word games and working crossword puzzles will help to improve his vocabulary skills. "Vocabulary development will be important as he progresses through school taking achievement tests such as ITBS, LEAP, ACT and SAT."

The Developmental Test of Visual Motor Integration showed Eric's visual-motor skills to be in the below-average range with a percentile rank of forty-five (45) and an age equivalent of eight years, nine months (8.9) which is below his chronological age. These results show that Eric could have difficulty performing some school-related tasks such as handwriting, copying information accurately from one source to another and/or interpreting information correctly from visual materials such as maps, charts and graphs. Also, he might experience difficulty with visual memory sequencing (such as inconsistent reversals of letters and numerals), faulty sequencing of letters in words and numbers in a series, disorder of events in life experiences as well as in written narrative, disorientation in time and space relationships and problems in processing, interpreting and recalling visual images.

The test of the oral pronunciation of graded sight words showed Eric's percentile rank at fifty-five (55) and a grade equivalent score of fourth grade, ninth month (4.9). Eric's age equivalent on this was nine years, nine months (9.9). Measuring his sight word recognition skill and his ability to automatically apply phonics skills to decode unfamiliar words, Eric's test results indicated that he was able to pronounce 127 of the 160 words on the primer through seventh grade list. More reading for pleasure would improve Eric's sight word vocabulary.

Eric read a series of graded passages on the oral reading inventory to determine his independent, instructional and frustrational levels of reading. "His comprehension was erratic, scoring at the independent, instructional and frustrational levels from the preprimer through the fourth grade passage." He had no difficulty with the oral reading of the passages, scoring at the independent level from the preprimer through the third grade passage and at the instructional level on the fourth grade passage.

On the vocabulary subtest of the Gates-MacGinitie Silent Reading Test, Eric

scored on a lower level than the other tests, rating at the second grade, sixth month level (2.6) with a percentile rank of eleven (11). Eric's comprehension subtest score was at second grade, fifth month level (2.5) with a percentile rank of twenty-two (22), and his total score on the silent reading test was at second grade, sixth month level (2.6) with a percentile rank of four (04). The rest results report said Eric would benefit from silent reading vocabulary and comprehension study to improve these skills which are critical skills needed in achievement testing.

Evaluation from Caddo Parish Pupil Appraisal Services (Office of Special Programs, Caddo Parish Schools) – December 1999

In the area of Reading, Eric's skills were tested in word recognition and comprehension. The recognition subtest measures the student's ability to identify specific letters and words, whereas the comprehension subtest requires a student to study a short passage that has a key word missing and determine a word appropriate to fit in the passage. Eric identified basic sight words, phonetically regular vocabulary and read passages at the fourth to fifth grade level with more difficult vocabulary. Inferential comprehension questions was where difficulty was noted. His fluency was good at fourth to fifth grade level, and his overall reading skills fell within the Above-Average range.

Computation skills and concepts were tested in the area of math. The math calculation subtest identifies a student's ability to perform mathematical calculations involving simple addition and subtraction to geometry and calculus. The ability to solve a practical math problem is tested through the applied problems/application section. Eric had the ability to complete problems requiring multiple digit addition and subtraction with regrouping, multiplication and division of simple numbers and computation of word problems with picture clues. Errors were found with Eric's inability to solve problems requiring addition of coins, multi-digit multiplication and division, computation of multi-step word problems or problem solving with time, money and measurement concepts. Difficulty was noted in Eric's ability to determine which process is needed to solve word problems. His overall math skills fell within the Average range.

Another area of the academic testing was in written language and spelling skills. In the dictation subtest, a student is required to spell single words with some requiring knowledge of capitalization, punctuation and plurals. In the writing samples subtest, the student is tested on his ability to write sentences and complete paragraphs using correct sentence structure and grammar. Eric successfully spelled basic sight words (two/three letter), spelled phonetically regular vocabulary words and wrote a compound sentence using correct capitalization and punctuation. However, he was unable to spell phonetically irregular vocabulary words or spell multisyllabic words correctly. If he had been able to study the words beforehand, however, he probably would have been able to memorize them and spell at least most of them correctly. He also had difficulty phrasing a sentence to answer a specific demand, but his sentences were mostly grammatically correct. In a sample of Eric's handwriting, he printed (his preferred way of writing), and his letters were generally formed correctly and legibility was fair. His overall written expression skills fell within the Average range.

The report summarized Eric's academic skills which ranged Average to Above Average. The report noted that Eric experiences difficulty in the classroom due to his inability to generalize directions and to identify the specific task to complete. His teachers have been providing classroom intervention appropriate to accommodate his needs.

One area of the test dealt with communication skills, was based on classroom observation and a review of academic skills and indicated that a speech impairment "significantly interferes" with educational performance in oral expression, listening comprehension and reading comprehension. The report said his teacher reported: "Eric had difficulty when trying to answer an oral question. He does well on written assignments, but has a hard time telling me an answer to a verbal question."

Eric was observed and screened informally with the results indicating his articulation, fluency and voice skills were within acceptable limits while he scored "at risk" in reasoning and pragmatic skills.

Examination of Eric's lips, tongue, teeth and hard and soft palates showed "an oral mechanism which appeared structurally and functionally adequate for speech production." However, the report noted, Eric wears braces and slightly distorts the "s" sound at times; therefore, articulation skills should be closely monitored. The speech and language sample results showed adequate sentence length and appropriate grammar skills.

Difficulty was noted in answering questions appropriately during conversational exchanges, and it was also noted that Eric does not understand some inferences and complex language. An example was given: "Are we going to finish the whole thing? We, uh, when it's time to go I have to finish a worksheet in my class."

Language skills were assessed through both formal and informal measures, and Eric "willingly entered the testing situation and completed all tasks. However, redirection was required due to Eric's apparent test anxiety and frequent inquiries about how long the testing would take." At least the language testing was performed during four different days at different times of the school day, and he didn't have to endure that much testing during one day. If so, there would have been many more questions from Eric about when testing would be over.

Eric was informally observed during two classroom situations which indicated some inability to comprehend implied meanings and directions. He followed the teacher's directions literally instead of making an appropriate inference. On occasion, the teacher would stand beside Eric and touch his paper to redirect him back on task. There were times when Eric would smile and make faces at his neighbor as well as put his fingers on his braces. With an increase in noise level in the classroom, Eric rocked on his stool and covered or rubbed his eyes. On one occasion, he covered his ears. During a group study time, Eric was observed studying alone.

Eric's raw score of 96 converted to a standard score of 80, a percentile of nine and an age equivalent of seven years, two months on the Peabody Picture Vocabulary Test-Third Edition (Form A). This test was given to measure single-word receptive (listening) vocabulary skills. Eric's score showed receptive vocabulary to be at least one standard deviation below the mean. The test was administered late in the school day, and the report noted this might have influenced Eric's score. If he was not sure of his answer, he would ask, "Is that right?"

Problem-solving and critical thinking skills were assessed by the Test of Problem Solving-Elementary, Revised. Eric was questioned on a broad range of critical thinking skills including clarifying, analyzing, generating solutions, evaluating and affective thinking. He earned a raw score of 32, or an age equivalency of six years, 0 months, with his performance indicating problem-solving skills to be greater than three standard deviations below the mean. To most "how" and "why" questions, Eric was unable to respond appropriately, and higher level vocabulary words were too difficult for Eric to define. He was unable to answer the questions, "What does destructive mean?" "What is a volunteer?" "What does recycling mean?"

A norm-referenced oral language assessment battery, known as the Comprehensive Assessment of Spoken Language, was given to assess Eric's basic language skills. Eric scored the following:

Subtests	Standard Scores
Antonyms	100
Syntax Construction	84

Paragraph Comprehension   79

Non-literal Language   87

Inference   80

Pragmatic Judgment   70

Eric's overall score fell at least one standard deviation below the mean, but his difficulty in pragmatic judgment and paragraph comprehension indicated a need for intervention.

A summary of this area of the test showed that Eric exhibits a "mild to moderate language disorder characterized by weaknesses in abstract reasoning, pragmatic skills and problem solving." Comprehension deficits are evident in the classroom, the report said, and recommended language therapy for remediation of complex language deficits, pragmatic and problem-solving skills and social language weaknesses.

The Boy Inside

About the Author

When someone meets Rhonda Jones Vardeman, it doesn't take long to realize that she's out-of-the-ordinary yet at the same time also very "normal" – in the best sense of both words. And when you read her book, you'll soon discover the same thing. Undoubtedly that's one of the reasons her son Eric, the subject of this book, is extraordinary – but is also just "a regular guy."

Eric, as the title indicates, is an Asperger's Syndrome success story. When Rhonda and her husband, Rob, discovered that Eric approached life differently from other children, they began a quest to discover why and to learn what they could do to help him. This book chronicles that journey – from birth to college. It's told from Rhonda's viewpoint, but is laced with Eric's own words as well as those of his therapist. The end result? A compelling narrative which shows that perseverance and conviction can overcome many obstacles ... that on oh-so-many levels success can be achieved.

True to Rhonda's nature, the story is related in a straight-forward manner with the attitude of "this is what happened to us, this is how we responded and this is what happened because of that." No preaching, no "one size fits all" mentality, just the story of one family and their special son.

Rhonda came to this project armed with a natural storyteller's art along with a journalism degree from Louisiana Tech University in Ruston, La. She honed those skills as an award-winning news reporter for the *Shreveport Journal* under the guidance of an editor who has since gone on to win a Pulitzer Prize. Other journalistic experience includes serving as editor of *Resource* and *Lagniappe* newsletters for Personnel Management, Inc., in Shreveport, La. She also has contributed freelance articles to magazines such as *River Cities, UpRiver* (suspense fiction),

Shreveport Magazine and *Blanchard Centennial*, a book commemorating 100 years of the town of Blanchard, La.

Adventuresome? Sure. She once went with two friends on a month-long camping trip from the Atlantic to the Pacific. Dedicated? You bet. Once she starts a project, you know you'll never have to worry about its being completed. Faithful? Absolutely. Her beliefs go to the core of her being and offer a stabilizing force in both her and her family's lives. Remarkable? Yes, but in the everyday sense that shows, really, if anyone puts her mind and efforts into a task, the result can be victory.

In the end, that's what this book is about. Eric inherited and absorbed many of these characteristics – from both Rhonda and Rob – and his parents helped to lead him along his successful journey. He couldn't have done it without them, but he also couldn't have done it without his own fortitude. The combination of those two things, in the words of Robert Frost, has made all the difference.

Sallie Rose Hollis

www.ingramcontent.com/pod-product-compliance
Lightning Source LLC
Chambersburg PA
CBHW021231090426
42740CB00006B/475